ART & DESIGN OF THE OLYMPIC GAMES

THE HISTORY OF THE

OLYMPIC GAMES

FASTER, HIGHER, STRONGER

Published in 2020 by Welbeck

An Imprint of Welbeck Non-Fiction Limited, part of Welbeck Publishing Group

20 Mortimer Street London W1T 3JW

© 2020 International Olympic Committee – All rights reserved

Design © Welbeck Non-Fiction Limited, part of Welbeck Publishing Group

First published by Carlton Books Limited in 2008

Editorial Director: Martin Corteel
Project Editor: Ross Hamilton
Design Manager: Luke Griffin

A CIP catalogue record for this book is available from the British Library

ISBN 978-1-78739-404-9

Printed in Dubai

10 9 8 7 6 5 4 3 2 1

ART & DESIGN OF THE OLYMPIC GAMES

THE HISTORY OF THE
OLYMPIC GAMES

FASTER, HIGHER, STRONGER

An official publication of the
Olympic Foundation for Culture and Heritage

WELBECK

CONTENTS

FOREWORD

When the Olympic Games Tokyo 2020 get underway, the eyes of the world will be on Japan. At the Olympic Games Tokyo 2020, the world will see athletes from all over the world and the IOC Refugee Olympic Team united in a celebration of unity in diversity of all humankind.

The Olympic spirit is returning to Tokyo for the second time, after 1964, and the stage is set for the most innovative Olympic Games in history. The Olympic Games Tokyo 2020 will be more youthful, more urban and more gender balanced. New urban sports will be on the programme that are popular with young people. In Tokyo, we will have effectively achieved gender balance with the highest-ever female athlete representation, at close to 49 per cent. The athletes will amaze the world with their achievements as they write a new chapter of sporting history. It is their performance, effort, excellence, and their emotions, that create the magic of the Olympic Games.

The History of the Olympic Games: Faster, Higher, Stronger chronicles the 124-year history and remarkable human adventure of the Games of the Olympiad, from the first modern Games in Athens in 1896 to these Games in Tokyo. Through its powerful storytelling, this publication brings to life the great moments of excellence, emotion and passion that make the Olympic Games so unique.

The diversity and richness of Olympic sport are treasures that we must, at the same time, preserve and share with future generations. This is what *The History of the Olympic Games: Faster, Higher, Stronger* is all about.

Thomas Bach
International Olympic Committee President

◀ The Olympic Games in Rio de Janeiro in 2016 showcased Brazil's diverse and thriving culture in a vibrant Opening Ceremony.

INTRODUCTION

The Olympic Games is the world's biggest sporting festival. The biggest in the numbers of its competitors, its spectators, and the global reach of its media coverage.

During its storied history of more than 100 years, the world's great cities have sought the right to host it and generations of men and women have willingly dedicated years of their lives in efforts to be part of its quadrennial celebrations.

Some have done so for the gold, silver and bronze medals and the prestige those bestow on their winners. Some only for the privilege and pleasure of taking part because, in the words of the Olympic Creed, "the important thing in life is not the triumph, but the fight; the essential thing is not to have won, but to have fought well".

All have played their part in ensuring that this modern adaptation of an ancient Greek festival, the brainchild of a French aristocrat seeking to promote the importance of sport in education, not only survives but continues to surpass itself in its success.

This book is a history of that evolution, a book of dreams, dedicated to the heroes and gallant losers, their triumphs and despair, and to an event that has become part of the fabric of the world, its five interlocking rings one of the most recognizable symbols across the globe.

In a unique association with The Olympic Museum and the International Olympic Committee, it seeks to bring to life the history of the Games and its participants through more than 200 photographs, artefacts and images of rare documents.

It shows how a Summer Games contested now by as many as 11,000 competitors in approximately 33 sports struggled for its first two decades just to stay alive. And through the Museum's collection it plots the remarkable transformation of the Games from its humble beginnings in Athens at the end of the 19th century, through to the stunning sporting spectacle it is now.

The Olympic Games are something quite unique. Its heroes walk proudly in the pantheon of sport, renowned and recognized in their lifetimes and remembered long after them.

Who has not heard of Jesse Owens and what he achieved, or of Paavo Nurmi, Mark Spitz and Olga Korbut? What child of a sporting nature has not watched in awe at the performances of Olympians and dreamed of emulating them, of standing on a podium with a medal around their necks and their national anthem playing?

What other event today, sporting or otherwise, projects its television coverage to 220 countries? What other has the potential to be viewed by more than 4 billion people?

This book is a record of a Games that continues its founder's work of bringing the youth of the world together every fourth year, a Games that, quite simply, is unique.

8

▶ The programme for the Opening Ceremony of the 1928 Amsterdam Olympic Games. At the ceremony, the team from Greece led the Parade of Nations, with the hosting Dutch team marching in last. Greece first, hosts last has been Olympic protocol ever since. The back cover features the Olympic motto: *Citius, Altius, Fortius* ("Faster, Higher, Stronger").

▶▶ The 1964 Olympic Games that took place in Tokyo were the first to be held in Asia. The last torch bearer of the flame, Yoshinori Sakai, was chosen because he was born on 6 August 1945, the day the atomic bomb exploded in Hiroshima, in homage to the victims and as a call for world peace. In 2020, the Games return to Tokyo once more.

CHAPTER 1

ANCIENT INSPIRATION AND EARLY MODERN FORM

On 23 June 1894, Baron Pierre de Coubertin saw the birth of his dream, to re-establish the ancient Olympic Games in a modern form. Coubertin's dream was slow to take shape though. Early editions, held first in Athens in 1896 and then every four years, were often months long and held alongside World's Fairs. The competition programme varied from edition to edition, but the foundations were being laid and the Games were becoming an event.

THE ANCIENT GAMES AND THE FOUNDING OF THE MODERN GAMES

Steeped in sporting and social history, the site of ancient Olympia and the Olympic Games that were introduced there more than 3,000 years ago undeniably served as a powerful inspiration to the founder of the modern Olympic Games, French nobleman Baron Pierre de Coubertin.

Whether it is 3,000 years ago or today, the site of ancient Olympia in Greece is revered as the home of the ancient Olympic Games. Located on the plain of Elis at the foot of Mount Kronios and the confluence of the Alpheios and Kladeos rivers, the site has a history that actually extends back to before the Games. Rediscovered in 1766, but not excavated until later, the site and its Olympic history subsequently fired the imagination of many individuals, including Baron Pierre de Coubertin.

The historical origin of the ancient Olympic Games as we know it today is like a puzzle, pieced together from a combination of still existing written records, artefacts discovered in the sanctuary and surrounding area as well as from myths. It is written records such as Pindar's odes and Hippias's list of Olympic victors from which a starting date of 776 B.C., evidence

of additions to the competitive events, and the exploits of the athletes are derived. Artefacts and remains of buildings show that the site and its surrounding area was inhabited and used for cult worship long before 776 B.C. Additionally, myths provide different stories of how and by whom the Games came to be introduced.

The ancient Olympic Games were not the only ones to be celebrated in Greece, but they were the most important. Held in honour of the god Zeus, their programme combined sporting competitions with religious ceremonies. The Games were celebrated once every four years and they were announced by heralds, *spondophoroi*, who travelled throughout the Greek empire to spread the news of the dates of the upcoming Games. It was also the role of the heralds to announce the sacred truce,

12

◀ 'Allégorie au Sport', an oil painting on canvas created by Charles de Coubertin in 1896. Charles Frédy, Pierre de Coubertin's father, was largely inspired by historical or religious subjects. This painting represents the crowning of athletes with the Erechteion temple and the Eiffel Tower in the background.

▲ Nudity was the rule for athletes while training. To protect themselves, they would rub themselves with oil and sprinkle themselves with fine sand. The oil was kept within a small flask or *aryballos* and tied to the wrist. This particular example dates from the first century.

the *ekecheiria*, that was designed to permit the safe passage
of athletes and spectators alike on their journey to and from
the Games.

The celebration that took place in 776 B.C. lasted only one
day and the sports part of the programme included only one
competition, a short footrace. The footrace, a *stade* or *stadion*
as it was named, was a sprint of one length of the stadium and it
was Koroibos of Elis who guaranteed his place in history as the
winner of that race. The *stade* remained the only event for the
first 13 editions of the Games.

The Games of 724 B.C. saw the first addition of an event
to the sports programme, the *diaulos*, another sprint which
was the length of two *stades*. Between 724 and 520 B.C. the
programme of sports competitions and, hand in hand with it,
the number of days of the Games expanded. The festivities
gradually increased, expanding from one to three and then finally
to five days in duration. The competitions also grew with the
additions of a pentathlon, boxing, wrestling, chariot races and
the *pankration*, a race in armour, and even a limited number of
events for boys. While females were not permitted to compete
they could, as an owner of an entry in a chariot race, still become
an Olympic champion.

At the Games, the victorious athlete received a simple crown
made from wild olive branches as his prize. Outside of the
Olympic sanctuary, however, the achievements of the athletes
were celebrated with gifts, odes and statues. For some, their
achievements were such that their fame lived on, even to today.

Among the most notable of these great athletes was Leonidas
of Rhodes, a winner of three running events at each of the four
consecutive Games between 164 and 152 B.C., an achievement

▼ In the eyes of artists, the Ancient Games
were as much a question of aesthetic grace
as accurate reportage: this 19th-century
engraving depicts a scene at Olympia,
imagined by the artist in the classical style
popular at the time.

▲ A vase depicting a *quadriga* or four-
horse chariot. According to the poet Pindar,
this type of race required competitors to
complete six laps, passing the posts at the
ends of the course a total of 12 times.

13

that was never surpassed at the ancient Olympic Games. The first man known to have won three events at a single celebration was Phanas of Pellene, in 512 B.C. Others remembered for their exploits also include Milon of Croton, who won six wrestling titles, and Belestiche of Macedonia. The owner of an entry in the four-horse chariot race for foals in 268 B.C., Belestiche is most often mentioned as the first example of a female winner of an ancient Olympic victor's title.

Despite all of these examples of impressive performances, the celebration of the ancient Olympic Games eventually became more sporadic and less significant during the period of Roman rule. Although it is uncertain precisely when the last Games were held, it is most commonly believed that their end is linked to the A.D. 393 edict of Theodosius I that ordered the closure of all pagan sites.

It was not until many centuries later that the Olympic Games again came to life under the guiding hand of Baron Pierre de Coubertin, this time in a modern form, on an international scale. Before Coubertin's proposal to re-establish the Olympic Games, however, there were other sporting competitions that drew from the examples of ancient Greek sports and

made use of the word 'Olympic'. One of the most well known of these examples was the Games that were held in Much Wenlock, England. Established in 1850 by Dr William Penny Brookes, these Games and the efforts of Penny Brookes served as yet another source of inspiration to Coubertin when he was formalizing his concept for a modern Olympic Games celebration.

Coubertin, an advocate of the use of sport as a means of education, saw the introduction of a modern version of the Games as a vehicle for promoting his theories, and first spoke publicly of them in a speech that he gave at the Sorbonne University in Paris in 1892. It would not, however, be until two years later, at an international conference at the Sorbonne where Coubertin again proposed his idea to re-establish the Games, that the idea was accepted. The conference's delegates not only gave their unanimous support to Coubertin's proposal but also agreed upon a date of 1896 and the host of Athens for the first celebration. They also approved the formation of an International Committee to guide their administration. Thus, on 23 June 1896 the link between ancient and modern was cemented and new Olympic history was made.

14

◄ The founder of the modern Olympic Games, Pierre de Coubertin. His primary aim was for sport to have a place at the heart of education and he saw the revival of the Olympic Games as a means of achieving this.

▶ A 1914 poster commissioned to celebrate the 20th anniversary of the Games restoration, it shows an athlete crowned with a laurel wreath and holding a statue of Nike, the goddess of Victory. The poster was designed by the Swiss painter Edouard Elzingre.

PIERRE DE COUBERTIN

Founder of the modern Olympic Games, Pierre de Frédy, Baron de Coubertin was a Frenchman who was keenly interested in reforming his country's education system in such a way as to put sport at its heart. The revival of an ancient sporting festival was secondary to him, a way of promoting his beliefs to a wider international audience.

Although his ideas on education never took root in France, the modern Olympic Games became his life's work. He was almost inseparable from his creation until 1925 when he resigned the presidency. So strong was his passion for his dream that he poured much of his money into seeing it realized and when he died in 1937, at the age of 74, his heart was buried near to the grounds of the Olympic sanctuary in ancient Olympia, Greece.

Commission des Jeux Olympiques

Séance du 19 Juin 1894
Présidence de M. D. Bikélas,
Délégué de la Société Panhellénique de gymnastique.

Le Président déclare la séance ouverte et remercie la Commission de l'honneur qu'elle a fait à la Grèce en le choisissant pour Président.

Il propose, comme préface aux délibérations de la Commission, de donner lecture d'un Mémoire remis par lui au Congrès, au nom de la Société panhellénique de gymnastique et relatif au rétablissement des jeux Olympiques. Cette proposition étant adoptée, Le Président donne lecture du mémoire en question, qui est écouté avec un vif intérêt.

L'auteur jette d'abord un coup d'œil sur les jeux olympiques tels qu'on les pratiquait dans l'antiquité; il fait remarquer que le concours le plus important était alors le pentathle En s'aqu'il consistait dans cinq exercices; pour ~~le pentathlon vainqueurs~~ il fallait exceller dans ces cinq exercices,

▲ Extract of the meeting of 19 June of the Minutes of the 1894 Athletic Congress of Paris showing the decision to re-establish the Olympic Games.

ATHENS 1896

Athletes from only 14 countries attended the Games, but so enthusiastic were the Greek people that the I Olympiad proved a great success.

◀ The cover of the official report on the 1896 Games, which listed the results and winners of each event.

▼ Featuring Athenian monuments, this was one of 12 Greek stamps issued to raise funds for the Games.

I OLYMPIAD

Opening date: 6 April 1896

Closing date: 15 April 1896

Country of host city: Greece (GRE)

Candidate cites: On 23 June 1894, at the first Olympic Congress which was held at the Sorbonne in Paris, the city of Athens was selected to host the Games of the I Olympiad

Nations: 14

Events: 43

▼ Participating athlete John Boland's diary of the 1896 Games.

◢ The Panathenian Stadium was reconstructed for the 1896 Games with marble throughout.

A typical participant of the I Olympiad was John Boland who was staying with an Athenian friend who was on the Organizing Committee. Boland's diary recalls how he entered the lawn tennis competition without any international experience and triumphed in the singles and doubles events.

From the moment the honour of hosting the first celebration of the modern Olympic Games was bestowed on the Greek capital, it was the enthusiasm of its public for the concept that drove the project to fruition.

A public appeal raised 332,756 drachma but it was the benevolence of George Averoff, a wealthy Greek businessman living in Egypt that won the day. He offered to pay the 920,000 drachma necessary to restore the ancient Panathenian Stadium.

Marbled throughout, the stadium was an impressive structure in spite of the tight turns and three laps to a kilometer dimensions of its running track that presented a challenge to the runners entered in the athletics competitions. A crowd of 40,000 filled it for the opening by King George I with a great many more on the surrounding hills which were said to have been a 'mass of humanity' that day.

Some of the other facilities were more makeshift. The swimming, for example, was held at sea with the competitors taken out in launches and then left in the water to swim back to shore. For the 1,200 metres race, the water was so rough and cold that the winner, Alfred Hajos, an 18-year-old Hungarian said: "My will to live completely overcame my desire to win."

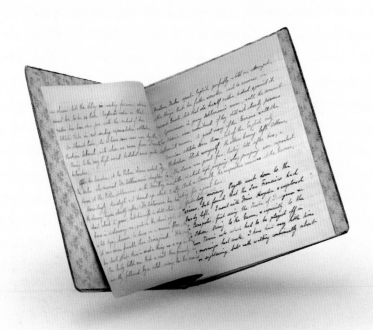

▲ These Princeton students returned home with an impressive haul. Herbert Jamison (below left) came second in 400 metres, Robert Garrett was victorious in the shot put, Albert Tyler came second in the pole vault and Francis Lane (above left) third in 100 metres.

Of a number of sports and events that were considered for inclusion in the programme a total of 43 events were ultimately held. Another seven rowing events were scheduled to take place but then had to be cancelled due to bad weather. Limited publicity for the Games outside Greece resulted in all but 90 of the 241 competitors being Greek. Many among the other 13 nationalities just happened to be in Athens and the Games were strictly only open to amateurs.

SPIRIDON LOUIS (GREECE)

When Spiridon Louis, a 24-year-old from a village near to Athens, won the first Olympic marathon, he entered Greek mythology. The expression in Greek 'egine Louis' came to mean 'run quickly'. The man himself, though, disappeared back into anonymity.

Athenians showered him with offers of gifts but he accepted only a horse and cart offered by the King. It replaced the mules from which he had previously made his living transporting barrels of fresh water twice a day to Athens, a probable reason for his great endurance.

He made one more appearance on the Olympic stage. In 1936, four years before his death, he was brought to Berlin to present a laurel wreath from the sacred grove at Olympia.

▶ Spiridon Louis, looking resplendent in traditional Greek costume. On winning the marathon, the public received him like an ancient hero.

Thirteen Americans from East Coast universities who travelled to compete arrived after a three-week journey only to discover that they had not taken into account the difference in the Greek and Julian calendars. Instead of 12 days in which to prepare for the Games, they opened the next afternoon! The surprise did them little harm as the Americans proved a great success in the athletics events. One, James Connolly, from Harvard, was to become the first Olympic champion of the modern era, winning the triple jump. He was awarded a silver medal and a crown of olive leaves, as were all winners. The medals were fashioned by a Frenchman, Jules Clément Chaplain and all medalists were given a prize diploma upon which was depicted a representation of Hellas, Nike and the ruins of the Parthenon. The designer of the diploma was Nicolas Gysis, a Greek artist living in Munich. The diploma was written in Greek as were the programme poster and the tickets to the events, all of which added to the atmosphere of the Greek setting of this first celebration of the Games.

There were no events for women and two events unknown in men's athletics at the time were created to link the Games with its ancient Greek ancestry: the discus and the marathon. The Greeks were disappointed when an American, Robert Garrett, won the throwing event, but of greater interest to them was the long race. No event of this distance was held at the ancient Olympic Games, but Michel Bréal, a Frenchman and friend of Pierre de Coubertin's, proposed it as a link with the legend of Pheidippides / Philippides running 25 miles from the village of Marathon to Athens to proclaim victory over the invading Persians in the Battle of Marathon in 490 B.C.

▼ Spiked leather shoes belonging to Angelo Bolanaki. He did not compete in 1896 but would later become an IOC member, first for Egypt and then for Greece.

▲ The 100 metres final was won in 12 seconds by the American Thomas Burke. It was Burke's second triumph of the Games – three days earlier he had won the 400 metre event.

In 1896 all but five of the 17 runners who set off from Marathon were Greek and a crowd estimated at 100,000 gathered in and around the stadium to welcome the anticipated Greek winner. Although there were several leaders throughout the course of the race, including the Australian Edwin Flack, winner of the 800 and 1,500 metres as well as a third place in tennis, it was a Greek, Spiridon Louis who would ultimately triumph. As Louis approached the end of the course, the cry 'Hellene! Hellene!' ('Greek! Greek!') could be heard, and when he arrived at the stadium the Princes George and Constantine were there to run the last lap with him.

COMITÉ INTERNATIONAL DES JEUX OLYMPIQUES

Conformément à la décision du Congrès international athlétique, réuni à Paris, au palais de la Sorbonne, du 15 au 23 juin 1894, les Jeux Olympiques vont être rétablis. Ils auront lieu désormais tous les quatre ans et successivement dans les grandes capitales du monde; le programme en sera exclusivement moderne et comprendra le tir, l'escrime, la gymnastique et les différents sports.

Les jeux seront inaugurés cette année à Athènes; leur seconde célébration aura lieu à Paris, en 1900; la troisième en 1904.

Les **Jeux olympiques de 1896** s'ouvriront à **Athènes** le lundi de Pâques, 6 avril.

A cette occasion, le Comité d'organisation institué à Athènes, sous la présidence de S. A. R. le Prince Royal de Grèce, prépare de grandes fêtes; l'enceinte du stade Panathénaïque, où auront lieu les courses à pied, a été restaurée aux frais d'un généreux Hellène. Un stand et un vélodrome ont été construits. Des excursions à Eleusis, Delphes et Olympie seront organisées pendant la période des jeux, qui prendront fin vers le 12 avril.

PROGRAMME DES JEUX

Le programme a été publié déjà par différents journaux; on peut le consulter au bureau du Comité, 229, rue Saint-Honoré; à l'Agence Cook, 1, Place de l'Opéra, ou aux Messageries Maritimes, 1, rue Vignon.

TRANSPORTS

1° Des billets à prix réduits, *valables 60 jours*, consentis par les Compagnies de Paris-Lyon-Méditerranée et des Messageries Maritimes, vont être mis en circulation aux conditions suivantes :

De Paris au Pirée et retour par Marseille (la nourriture comprise à bord des paquebots).

Ligne de Constantinople. Départ : le *samedi*, tous les 14 jours : 7 mars, 21 mars, 4 avril (classe unique de chambre).

Prix : **300 francs** en 1re *Classe*.

Ligne de Syrie (départ : le *jeudi*, tous les 14 jours : 12 mars, 26 mars, 9 avril).

Prix : **340 francs** en 1re classe. **230 francs** en 2e classe.

Les paquebots de Constantinople contiennent 26 places seulement.

Les paquebots de Syrie » 116 » de 1re et 100 de 2e.

2° En outre, un paquebot spécial, *Le Sénégal*, doit partir de Marseille le 29 mars prochain, et effectuer le parcours suivant :

1er avril. — Arrivée à *Katakolo* (excursion à Olympie).
2 » — » à *Itéa* » à *Delphes*).
3 » — » à *Nauplie* » à *Argos, Mycènes, Epidaure*).
5 » — » au *Pirée* (*Athènes*).
6, 7, 8 » — *Séjour à Athènes* (*Jeux olympiques*).
9 » — Arrivée à *Délos* (escale à *Syra*).
10 au 13 » — *Retour à Marseille*.

Les excursions seront dirigées par des Elèves et anciens Elèves de l'Ecole d'Athènes.

Les inscriptions sont reçues au siège de la Compagnie des Messageries Maritimes, 1, rue Vignon, au bureau des Passages. La liste provisoire sera close le 24 février.

Les dames sont admises. *Le Sénégal* recevra 216 passagers.

Le prix du voyage de Marseille à Marseille, tout compris, même les repas pendant la durée des escales, est fixé à

450 francs en 1re classe. **380 francs** en 2e classe.

3° Enfin un départ supplémentaire pour le Pirée pourra avoir lieu vers la date du *mardi* 31 mars, si 200 passagers en font la demande. Ces demandes doivent être adressées, *avant le 10 mars*, à la Compagnie des Messageries Maritimes, qui y donnera suite s'il y a lieu.

SÉJOUR A ATHÈNES

Pour les conditions de séjour à Athènes, s'adresser à l'agence Cook. Une commission de « Réception des Etrangers » a été constituée à Athènes, par le Comité d'organisation.

RENSEIGNEMENTS

Pour les demandes de renseignements supplémentaires concernant les jeux, s'adresser directement à M. Philémon, ancien maire d'Athènes, secrétaire général du Comité d'organisation. Athènes.

Paris, le 1er Février 1896.

Le Secrétaire du Comité Français, *Le Secrétaire Général du Comité International,*
R. FABENS. Baron Pierre de COUBERTIN.

◀ Official information poster for the athletes, officials and general public wishing to go to Athens.

▲ Prize diploma designed by Nikolaus Gysis. It includes a representation of Hellas, Nike and the ruins of the Parthenon. The artist was influenced by the Jugendstil and his style goes from tradition to modernity.

◀ A first place winner's medal designed by Jules Clément Chaplain, a well-known artist of this time. The obverse features Zeus's face along with a globe with winged victory on it. First place winners were awarded this silver medal, an olive branch and a diploma. Those in second place were given a copper medal, a branch of laurel and a diploma.

▶ In winning the triple jump, America's James Connolly became the first Olympic champion of the modern era.

JAMES CONNOLLY (UNITED STATES)

The American national champion in triple jump, Connolly, an undergraduate at Harvard, was refused permission by his Dean to take a leave of absence from his studies to compete in the Olympic Games. So he dropped out of his course and arrived, minus his wallet, which was stolen in Naples, less than 24 hours before his event.

He won the triple jump by more than a metre, took third place in the long jump and tied with Robert Garrett for second in the high jump, an event won by another Harvard undergraduate, Ellery Clark. Years later, after becoming a noted war correspondent and author of 25 novels, he declined when Harvard offered him an honorary degree.

PARIS 1900

Pierre de Coubertin's dream of hosting the Games in his native city did not work out as planned but nonetheless their celebration in Paris contributed an interesting new chapter to Olympic history.

◀ A poster created by Jean Pal (Jean de Paleologu) for the fencing competitions. Although it shows a woman, no females participated in the fencing events. Similar posters were created for some of the events such as athletics, rowing, cycling and gymnastics.

II OLYMPIAD

Opening date: 14 May 1900

Closing date: 28 October 1900

Country of host city: France (FRA)

Candidate cities: None

Nations: 24

Events: 95

▼ New Yorker John Flanagan won the first of his hammer titles in Paris.

When, in 1894 at the first Olympic Congress at the Sorbonne, Baron Coubertin presented his idea to re-establish the Olympic Games he had it in his mind that Paris would play host to the first celebration in 1900. His idea was unanimously accepted but enthusiasm was such that the delegates of the Congress decided on an earlier start date and a different place. Thus, Paris became the second host of the modern Olympic Games in 1900 and Athens the first in 1896.

Unlike the Games in Athens, those in Paris became an adjunct to a World's Fair, the 'Universal Exposition', and were stretched over a far longer period of time, running from May to October 1900. Coubertin's original vision to create a sporting stage in the heart of Paris based on the theme of ancient Olympia, complete with pillars and statues, was, however, lost amidst the tug-of-war that ensued between the World's Fair organizers and the Baron.

The impact of this struggle is evident in the artefacts and documents that remain from these Games. It was more common to see the words 'Exposition Universelle' rather than the word 'Olympic' on items such as the posters, tickets, medals or souvenirs. One document used the title 'Programme of the Olympic Games of 1900' and listed certain events and another referred to the sporting contests as 'Competitions of Physical Exercise and Sport'. It is no wonder then that some spectators and competitors may not have realized which of the two international events they were witnessing or participating in or that some historians today debate which events were and were not Olympic.

When the Opening Ceremony for the Fair was held in April 1900 there was no mention of the Games. A month later when the Olympic events got under way they did so without any further ceremony. None of this, however, prevented the athletes from putting on a show of their own, demonstrating their sporting prowess and creating new Olympic history.

For women, history was quickly made even before the competitions had started, as 1900 marked the first time participation of female athletes at the Games. Participation alone was not the only thing historic about the inclusion of women as their performances also made history, and the legends of some of these women live on to this day.

Charlotte Cooper of Great Britain, for example, not only became the first Olympic tennis champion in the women's

▲ This silver prize plaque was created by Frédéric Vernon. This medal was presented for the gymnastics event.

▲ A cup showing the Eiffel Tower and six monuments of the Paris World's Fair. There is no mention of the Olympic Games.

21

▶ Raymond 'Ray' Ewry won a gold medal in the now defunct standing jump event.

▲ Cigarette cards issued by Hassan, celebrating victorious athletes Ray Ewry and John Flanagan from the 1900 Games.

▼ Entry ticket for the Paris World's Fair.

RAY EWRY (UNITED STATES)

Ray Ewry, from Lafayette, Indiana, was an unlikely contender for Olympic glory. He contracted polio as a child and was confined to a wheelchair amid doubts that he would ever walk again. He proved the doubters wrong, first doing leg exercises and then when he could walk again he strengthened his legs by jumping.

Nicknamed 'the Human Frog', he became the greatest exponent of the standing jumps – the long, the high and the triple – winning all three events at the Games in both 1900 and 1904 as well as the standing high jump and the standing long jump in London in 1908. In 1912, at almost 40 years of age he only narrowly missed making the American team for a fourth Olympic Games.

CHARLOTTE COOPER (GREAT BRITAIN)

Charlotte Cooper, nicknamed 'Chattie', was a tall, elegant Londoner who played tennis wearing the ankle-length dresses of the time which disguised her power about the court. She dominated tennis at the turn of the 20th century, winning three women's singles titles at Wimbledon before she competed at the Olympic Games in 1900. She won a further two Wimbledon titles following Paris and was also a five time runner-up at that tournament during her sporting career.

Her final victory at Wimbledon, several years after she had started a family, came at the age of 37. She died at the age of 96 in 1966.

▲ Charlotte Cooper serves during the women's singles tennis event at the 1900 Games, in which she won gold.

➤ A style of wooden tennis racket that was used between 1870 and 1910. Flutes on the handle were sculpted to reduce sweat. At the turn of the century, the 'fishtail' was created to prevent the hand from slipping.

singles event but also collected a second gold in the mixed doubles event. Meanwhile, American Margaret Abbott, who just happened to be in Paris, took the opportunity to play a round of golf and went home an Olympic champion, although she did not know it. For Abbott and her mother Mary, who also competed and finished in a tie for 7th place, had simply entered an international golf tournament that was part of the Fair. For Olympic historians, though, Abbott's performance earned her

place in the records books as the first women's Olympic golf champion and the first American woman to win an Olympic gold medal.

Amongst the men there were also a number of notable performances. In athletics there was Alvin Kraenzlein who had victories in the 60 metres, 110 and 200 metres hurdles and the long jump, a feat not since surpassed by any other athlete in the individual events in his sport. Another individual star was Ray

Ewry who made an impressive entry into the Olympic arena by winning all three of the standing jump events in a single day.

The challenge presented by the avenue of trees in the Bois de Boulogne where the hammer throw competition was held did little to prevent the eventual winner, New Yorker John Flanagan from later being celebrated in a series of cigarette cards, one of the first examples of an Olympian's image being used for merchandising.

In addition to the performances of the athletes, the Games of 1900 were also notable for the introduction of several sports that have since disappeared from the Olympic programme. These included golf, rugby (both of which returned at the 2016 Games) and polo, as well as perhaps, slightly ironically, a tug-of-war competition. In the case of the tug-of-war event it was a combined team from Sweden and Denmark that won the gold.

In the case of the broader Olympic picture though it was Pierre de Coubertin who ultimately triumphed over the tug-of-war that had been waged with the organizers of the World's Fair as despite all the ups and downs the Games survived to be staged again four years later.

▲ A decorative plate by Heinrich Kautsch from Bohemia. It was a timid step towards the stylistic vocabulary of the new century, Art Nouveau.

◀ An early proposal for the programme of events for the 1900 Olympic Games which lists the members of the International Olympic Committee and the sports to be contested which included athletics, fencing, gymnastics and cycling, as well as team sports including cricket and rugby.

PROGRAMME
DES
JEUX OLYMPIQUES DE 1900
⟶ PARIS ⟵

Comité International des Jeux Olympiques:

Président . . . . M. le Baron PIERRE DE COUBERTIN . . . . Paris.

MEMBRES. MM. Lord AMPTHILL . . . Londres.   MM. le Docteur W. GEBHARDT . . . Berlin.
Le Commandant V. BALCK . . . Stockholm.   le Docteur JIRI GUTH . . . Prague.
D. BIKELAS . . . Athènes.   C. HERBERT . . . Londres.
Le Comte BRUNETTA d'USSEAUX . . . Turin.   Fr. KEMENY . . . Budapest.
Le Comte M. DE BOUSIES . . . Bruxelles.   W. M. SLOANE . . . New-York.
Le Général DE BOUTOWSKI . . . Saint-Pétersbourg.   Le Baron F. W. DE TUYLL . . . Velsen (Pays-Bas).
E. CALLOT . . . Paris.   J. B. ZUBIAUR . . . Concepcion del Uruguay
I. A. CUFF . . . Christ Church (N.-Zélande).   (Rép. Argentine).

Comité d'Organisation des Jeux Olympiques de 1900

Président : M. le Vicomte de la ROCHEFOUCAULD.   Secrétaire général : M. Robert FOURNIER-SARLOVÈZE.

MEMBRES. MM. le Comte PHILIPPE d'ALSACE.   MM. le Comte CHANDON DE BRIAILLES.   MM. le Duc de LORGE.
G. BAUGRAND.   le Marquis de CHASSELOUP-LAUBAT.   Frédéric MALLET.
* le Baron JEAN DE BÉLLET (Lawn-Tennis).   * M. DUBONNET (Aviron).   * le Comte F. DE MAILLÉ (Vélocipédie).
le Cte A. DE BERTIER DE SAUVIGNY (Tir à l'arc).   R. DUPUYTREM, député.   F. DE NEUFVILLE.
P. DE BOULOGNE (Yachting).   le Comte d'ESTERNO.   ARTHUR O'CONNOR (Courte Paume).
* Georges BOURDON (Sports athlétiques).   le Baron ANDRÉ DE FLEURY.   * le Comte N. POTOCKI (Escrime).
BOUSSOD.   ALFRED GALLARD.   le Comte JACQUES DE POURTALÈS (Golf).
le Duc de BRISSAC.   * le Comte A. DE GUÉBRIANT (Yachting).   * CH. RICHEFEU (Longue Paume).
* BRUNEAU DE LABORIE (Boxe).   Gordon BENNETT.   ANDRÉ TOUTAIN.
* E. CAILLAT (Aviron).   J. J. JUSSERAND.   le Comte TURQUET DE LA BOISSERIE.
Charles CAMBEFORT.   le Baron LA CAZE.   * Hérrand DE VILLENEUVE (Escrime).
le Baron DE CARAYON LA TOUR.   * le Baron LEJEUNE (Polo).

N. B. — Les Noms des Commissaires sportifs sont précédés d'une astérisque. Les Commissaires pour la gymnastique, la natation, le foot-ball, etc... seront ultérieurement nommés.

Programme des Jeux

Sports athlétiques. — *Courses à pied* - 100 m., 400 m., 800 m., 1500 mètres (courses plates), 110 mètres (courses de haies).
Concours : Sauts en longueur et en hauteur (running long and high jumps).
Saut à la perche (Pole vault).
Lancement du poids (Putting the weight) et du disque.
Pentathle (Championnat général d'athlétisme), 4 épreuves: 100 ou 400 m., 800 ou 1500 mètres. — Saut en hauteur, en longueur ou à la perche. — Lancement du poids ou du disque.
(Règlements de l'Union des Sociétés françaises des Sports athlétiques).
Gymnastique. — *Exercices individuels* — Corde lisse en traction des bras. — Rétablissements divers à la barre fixe. — Mouvements aux anneaux. — Barres parallèles profondes. — Saut au cheval. — Travail des poids.
Escrimes. — Assauts de fleuret, de sabre et d'épée. — (Amateurs, Professeurs civils et militaires). — (Règlements de la Société d'Encouragement de l'Escrime).
Assauts de boxe anglaise et de boxe française.
Assauts de canne et de bâton.
Lutte : suisse et romaine.
Sports nautiques. — *Yachting* : Courses à la voile en rivière (Yachts au-dessous de 8 tonneaux). — Courses à la voile en mer (Yachts de 20 tonneaux).
Règlements du Cercle de la Voile de Paris et de l'Union des Yachts français).
Aviron : Un rameur : 2000 mètres sans virage (Skiffs).
Deux rameurs de pointe : 2400 mètres sans virage (Outriggers).
Quatre rameurs »
Huit rameurs »

Natation : Courses de vitesse : 100 mètres.
fond et vitesse : 500 mètres.
fond : 1000 mètres.
Concours de plongeon et de sauvetage.
Water-Polo.
Vélocipédie. — Course de vitesse : 2000 m., sur piste, sans entraîneurs.
Course de fond : 100 kilomètres, sur piste, avec entraîneurs. (L'entraînement mécanique sera prohibé).
Courses de tandems : 3000 mètres, sur piste, sans entraîneurs.
Sport hippique. — *Polo* (Règlements des Clubs de Hurlingham et Paris).
Jeux. — *Foot-Ball* (Rugby et Association).
Cricket.
Golf (Règlements de Saint-Andrews, modifié selon les nécessités locales).
Lawn-Tennis (simple et double).
Croquet.
Hockey.
Longue-Paume.
Courte-Paume.
Alpinisme. — Un prix olympique sera décerné à l'auteur de l'ascension la plus remarquable accomplie sur un point quelconque du globe depuis la célébration des Jeux olympiques de 1896.
Tir à l'arc. — (Un règlement de concours est à l'étude.)
Patinage. —   id.

N. B. — Conformément aux décisions fondamentales du Congrès International de 1894, les Concours olympiques sont réservés aux seuls amateurs répondant aux définitions adoptées par l'Union des Sports athlétiques, l'Amateur Athletic Association d'Angleterre et les autres Sociétés d'Amateurs du monde.
Les concours sont tous des championnats.
Les dates et lieux des concours ainsi que les dates de clôture des engagements, bien que déjà fixés, seront publiés ultérieurement, le Comité d'organisation se réservant d'introduire, s'il y a lieu, quelques modifications dans cette partie du programme.
Les prix consisteront en objets d'art, exclusivement.

Toutes les communications relatives aux **Jeux olympiques de 1900**, doivent être adressées :
17, Rue de Varennes — Paris.

PARIS. — IMP. A. QUELQUEJEU, RUE GERBERT, 10.   AFFICHE D'INTÉRIEUR.

▲ Alvin Kraenzlein was the only track and field athlete to win gold medals in four individual events. He won the 60 metres, the 110 metres hurdles and the 200 metres hurdles together with the long jump.

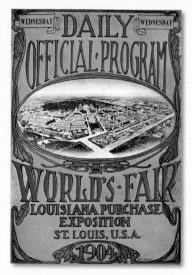

ST. LOUIS 1904

The first Olympic Games to be held outside Europe, they were absorbed into the St. Louis World's Fair. The sporting competitions, both Olympic and non-Olympic, stretched over five months running from July to November 1904.

◀ The cover of the official programme in 1904 focused only on the concurrently running World's Fair in St. Louis and not the Olympic Games.

III OLYMPIAD

Opening date: 1 July 1904
Closing date: 23 November 1904
Country of host city: United States (USA)
Candidate city: Chicago (USA). Chicago was chosen initially but it was decided to transfer to St Louis after a vote of 14 for and 2 against)
Nations: 12
Events: 91

▶ American Frederick Winters shows his strength in the dumbbell competition. He would go on to finish second in the one-hand lift.

▼ The eventual winners of the tug-of-war event were the American team, who were made up mostly of the Milwaukee Athletic Club athletes.

In 1904, the Olympic Games were once again held in conjunction with another event. Originally designated by the IOC to take place in Chicago, the shift of the St. Louis World's Fair, officially known as the Louisiana Purchase Exposition, from the year 1903 to 1904 changed Olympic history. When, in reaction to the St. Louis decision to shift dates, the Chicago organizers proposed moving the Olympic celebration to 1905, the idea to break with the four-year period of the Olympiad was not viewed as an acceptable solution by Pierre de Coubertin. Thus, when it became evident that the Olympic Games might suffer from competition with the World's Fair and the athletics events that its organizers were adamant about planning, the decision was made that the 1904 Games should be shifted to St. Louis.

When the hosting role of the Games was reassigned to St. Louis they became absorbed into the plans for the celebration of the Exposition. So complete was the absorption and so limited are the existing documents that could shed light on the history of this Olympic celebration that, to this day, there is still debate over which events were Olympic and which were not. For some, such as boxing, dumbbells, freestyle wrestling and the decathlon, the IOC approval that was given in 1901 for their inclusion in the Games make it clear that they were Olympic. Others such as

CHARLES 'ARCHIE' HAHN (UNITED STATES)

The son of a tobacconist in Dodgeville, a small farming town in Wisconsin, Hahn never set foot on a track until he was 19. His high school did not have a track team and in spite of his diminutive size he played on its football team instead.

One year after his track debut representatives from the University of Michigan who were in attendance at a county fair saw Hahn run and were so impressed by his win there that they offered him a scholarship and he was to be sprint champion of the 'Big Ten' colleges for four years. He won Canadian and US national titles in 1903 and, after his three wins in St Louis, won the 100 again at the Intercalated Games in Athens in 1906. He then turned professional, running in stunts at county fairs including beating a racehorse over 50 yards, before later coaching track and football teams at some of America's most prestigious colleges until the age of 70.

◄ American Marcus Hurley proved to be a formidable opponent as he cycled his way to four golds and one bronze at the Games in St. Louis.

▲ Baron de Coubertin's letter to US President Theodore Roosevelt concerning Chicago's election as the host city for the 1904 Olympic Games.

athletics, fencing, and swimming were also again clearly on the sports programme. Olympic or not, and possibly lost amongst the celebration of the World's Fair, the competitions nonetheless provided several memorable, unexpected and historic Olympic moments, most notably in the athletics competitions.

The number three best described the results both on the athletics running track and the field, as performers such as the American Ray Ewry demonstrated their athletic prowess with triple victories. For Ewry it was a repeat of Paris, as he again came away with gold medals in all three of the standing jumps. Other triple winners were Charles 'Archie' Hahn, dubbed 'the Milwaukee Meteor', who won the 60, 100 and 200 metres and Harry Hillman, who proved that hurdles were not an obstacle by winning both the 200 and 400 metres hurdles along with the 400 metres race.

Athletics also provided another unexpected triple and several Olympic firsts. The surprise belonged to James Lightbody, a 22-year-old from Chicago who dominated the middle-distance events. Competing for his first ever time in the steeplechase, Lightbody scored another more personal first by taking away the gold medal. In the days that followed he won the 800 metres in an Olympic record time as well as the 1,500 metres. Two bronze medal finishes in the 200 and 400 metres hurdles distinguished George Poage as the first African American to win medals at the Olympic Games and the marathon entrants included Len Tau and Jan Mashiani, the first black African competitors.

The 1904 marathon is also remembered for a ride in a car rather than running. As temperatures soared to 32°C the race became a survival test which only 14 of 32 runners finished. It was originally thought that the American Fred Lorz was the victor and his compatriot Thomas Hicks was the second place finisher until it was discovered that Lorz had accepted a ride in an automobile and only run part of the distance. Lorz was banned for life but the suspension was lifted shortly thereafter and he would go on to

26

▲ Omitted from Athens on grounds that it was dangerous, Olympic boxing appeared in St. Louis thanks to its popularity in the United States. These gloves belonged to IOC President Pierre de Coubertin, also a practitioner of the sport.

◀ Although winner of the marathon, Thomas Hicks was not the first to cross the line he was crowned champion.

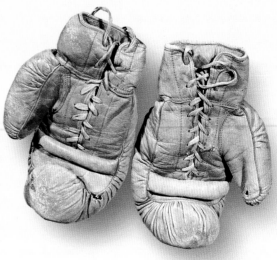

▲ Winner's medal manufactured by Dièges & Clust, New York. The design of both sides was probably inspired by the medal of the 1896 Athens and 1900 Paris Games. The reverse shown here represents a winged victory on the globe and the bust of Zeus.

win the 1905 Boston marathon. It would be Hicks, however, who would take home Olympic gold.

Memorable athletics performances were balanced by equally memorable performances in other sports such as gymnastics where Anton Heida won five golds and one silver and George Eyser proved almost as formidable despite having a wooden leg, winning three golds, two silvers and one bronze medal. Frank Kungler put on an impressive display in the strength events competing not only in the newly introduced dumbbells event but also in freestyle wrestling and on one of the tug-of-war teams. He would come away with medals in all four events he competed in, one silver and three bronze.

The highlights of the 1904 Games would not be complete without also mentioning the awards. For the first time, the first through to third place athletes in each event received a medal, so it is the tradition of gold for first, silver for second and bronze for third that we can thank the organizers of St. Louis for.

▶ The Chicago athlete James 'Jim' Lightbody achieved great success in St. Louis winning the 800 metres, 1,500 metres and 2,500 metres.

◀ A gold-plated Art Nouveau badge issued to commemorate the St. Louis World's Fair.

◢ A French promotional poster for the St. Louis World's Fair created by the famous Art Nouveau designer Alphonse Mucha. It shows a female figure and a Native American.

MEYER PRINSTEIN (UNITED STATES)

At the 1900 Olympic Games in Paris, Meyer Prinstein looked like a good bet for gold in the long jump following the qualifying round. Unfortunately, although he was Jewish, he was prohibited by an official from his university from competing in the final on the Sunday. Nonetheless his qualifying jump of 7.175 metres on the Saturday earned him second place based on the rules of the time that stipulated that the results of the qualifying round could be counted in the final placing. He would also win a gold medal in the triple jump.

Four years later there was nothing stopping Prinstein and he won both the long and triple jump events and was fifth in both 60 and 400 metres. He then travelled to Athens for the Intercalated Games of 1906 where he beat the new world record holder, Ireland's Peter O'Connor, with his first jump.

LONDON 1908

Built for the Olympic Games, the White City Stadium was a centerpiece of the celebrations. With its multifunctional design it played host to a large majority of the sports on the programme for the Games.

IV OLYMPIAD

Opening date: 27 April 1908

Closing date: 31 October 1908

Country of host city: Great Britain (GBR)

Candidate cities: Berlin (GER), Milan (ITA), Rome (ITA) Rome was chosen initially, but the Games were subsequently reattributed to London

Nations: 22

Events: 110

► This jewelry box was produced to commemorate the 1908 Games and the Franco-British exhibition.

►► Programme and route guide to the Great Marathon Race.

◢ A railway promotional poster. It shows an athlete holding a flag with the White City Stadium which was built specifically for the Games appearing in the background.

◄ The cover of the official programme for the 1908 Games, which highlighted the new stadium built at Shepherd's Bush.

▼ Competitor's badge manufactured by Vaughton. This badge shows the profile of the goddess Athena and a branch of laurel. Different badges allowed for people to be categorized by their function – for example, referee, official, athlete, etc. This system made it easier to identify officials and staff who did not wear uniforms at this time.

When the host city for the Games of the IV Olympiad was chosen in 1904 the city of London was not even a candidate. Nonetheless, two years later, when Rome bowed out due to financial reasons, it was London that the IOC approached to take over. On 19 November 1906 the IOC was informed that London was willing to take up the challenge.

Like today, most of the competition schedule of London was concentrated around the Opening ceremony on 13 July 1908 and the roughly two week period that followed. Unlike today, however, events such as racquets, jeu de paume and polo were also held in advance and sports considered more autumn or winter based such as rugby football, lacrosse and even figure skating were held later.

Thus, the Games dates spread from April to October. In selecting the venues for the competitions, the Organizing Committee made use of existing and well known facilities such

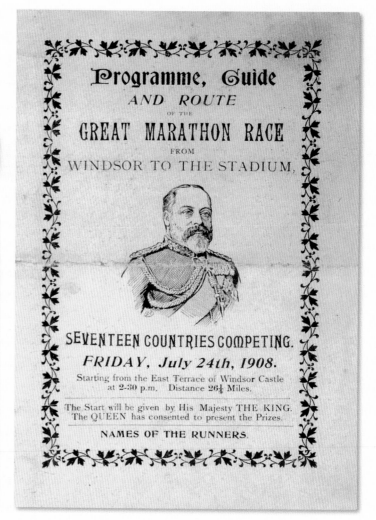

as Henley-on-Thames for the rowing and Wimbledon for tennis. It was also necessary for certain events to be held further afield with Glasgow and the Isle of Wight serving as the sites for the yachting competitions and Southampton Waters off the south coast of England being used for motor boat races.

Of all the venues that were used for the Games, it was the White City Stadium at Shepherd's Bush in West London that became a centerpiece of the Games. The stadium was built at no cost to the British Olympic Association by the organizers of the Franco-British Exhibition. In exchange, an agreement was made that the Franco-British Exhibition organizers would receive a percentage of the proceeds from the sale of admission tickets. The stadium design was uniquely multifunctional with a 100 metres swimming pool within a running track embraced by a cycling oval and seating for a capacity crowd of more than 66,000.

The pool proved to be notable not only because of its location in the infield of the running track and the winning ways of athletes such as triple gold medalist Henry Taylor of Great Britain. It was also the first time that Olympic swimming competitions were held in a pool.

In the track events, debate over the rules would lead to an Olympic first and last when only one athlete showed up for the re-run of the 400 metres final. In the absence of the two Americans who had also qualified to take part but in protest of the re-run refused, British athlete Wyndham Halswelle ran the race alone and took gold.

29

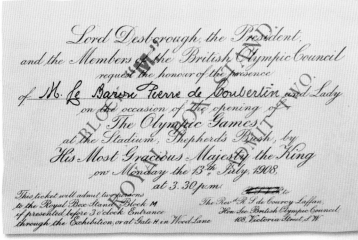

◀ Baron de Coubertin's personal invitation to the Royal Box to watch the Opening Ceremony.

▶ Wyndham Halswelle was the victor in what turned out to be a rather unique Olympic race finish.

▼ Field hockey made its first appearance in 1908. This is the Great British goalkeeper H. I. Woods' cap, whose team won gold.

WYNDHAM HALSWELLE (GREAT BRITAIN)

Lieutenant Wyndham Halswelle, a Londoner of Scottish descent, was a veteran of the Boer War who fought in four battles. He took up athletics in 1904, when already 22, but was immediately successful. In 1905 he won the Scottish and Amateur Athletic Association 440-yard championships and in 1906 he won four titles on a single day at the Scottish championships.

His infamous victory in the 1908 Olympic Games so dismayed him that after one more race he retired from competition. He was later promoted to captain but died in 1915 in the First World War trying to rescue another wounded officer.

On a more positive note, the flexibility in the setting of the rules made it possible for the British organizers to introduce the Olympic marathon as we know it today, a race of 26 miles 385 yards (42,195 metres). The change of distance allowed for its start on the East Lawn at Windsor Castle and finish in the White City stadium directly in front of the Royal box.

The running of this particular Olympic marathon is perhaps even better known as the Italian Dorando Pietri's race – even though Pietri did not actually win the gold medal. Although Dorando did make it across the finish line first, it was the exhausted and dramatic way in which he did that led to his eventual disqualification for receiving assistance so the gold medal was awarded to American runner John Hayes.

In the shooting competitions Swedish athlete Oscar Swahn made his first Olympic appearance. In 1908 Swahn took home two golds in the running deer single shots individual and team events as well as a bronze in the running deer double shots individual event. He would go on to win one more medal of each colour in his subsequent Games, the last in Antwerp 1920, and to this day he holds the distinction of being the oldest athlete at 64, male or female, to have won an Olympic gold medal.

Olympic Games history of another kind was also realized in 1908. A special religious ceremony linked to the celebration that took place on 12 July 1908 proved equally special to Pierre de Coubertin. Based on a sermon that was given there by the Bishop of Pennsylvania, Ethelbert Talbot, Coubertin would subsequently write the words that were to become the Olympic creed of the modern Olympic Games. "The important thing in life is not the triumph, but the fight; the essential thing is not to have won, but to have fought well."

▲ As part of the IV Olympiad in London a number of winter sports competitions were organized including figure skating events for men, women and pairs.

◣ Dorando Pietri, the disqualified but ultimately celebrated Italian marathon runner. He would later be received by royalty.

▼ Profile photographs of Dorando Pietri and John Hayes with details of the dramatic outcome in the marathon.

30

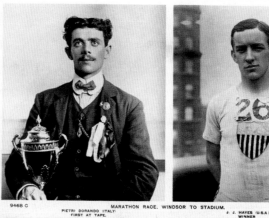

9468 C   MARATHON RACE. WINDSOR TO STADIUM.
PIETRI DORANDO (ITALY)   J. J. HAYES (U.S.A.)   ROTARY PHOTO, E.C.
FIRST AT TAPE.   WINNER

DORANDO PIETRI (ITALY)

Dorando Pietri is perhaps best known for the 1908 race he struggled to finish instead of those he did. He may not have won an Olympic gold in London but a sympathetic crowd took him to their hearts. Additionally, the Queen summoned him the day after the event to receive a gold cup and race promoters in America invited him to turn professional.

He twice beat Olympic champion Johnny Hayes in professional marathons, was unbeaten in 10 competitions in 1910, two against horse-ridden opponents, and retired the following year having won 50 of his 69 professional races.

◀ Winner's medal designed by Bertram MacKennal. The obverse shows two young women crowning the victorious athlete. The reverse features a winged victory and Saint George, England's patron saint, killing a dragon.

▼ Johnny Hayes, although the second marathon runner to cross the line, he was the first to do it unassisted. Here, he is carried on a table after being proclaimed the rightful winner.

▲ The Canadian Robert Kerr is lifted aloft following his victory in the 200 metres sprint.

▼ Henry Taylor celebrates after coming first in the 4 x 200 metres swimming freestyle.

STOCKHOLM 1912

The Games of the V Olympiad were a celebration marked by the introduction of a number of notable technical, artistic and Olympic competition firsts.

V OLYMPIAD

Opening date: 5 May 1912

Closing date: 27 July 1912

Country of host city: Sweden (SWE)

Candidate cities: None

Nations: 28

Events: 102

◀ First official poster issued for an Olympic Games. It represents a procession of athletes each carrying their national flag. The artwork was slightly modified for the poster to lessen the emphasis on the athlete's nakedness and corrected for the representation of the flags but nonetheless it was still not used for advertising in certain countries.

▶ A competitor's badge featuring Athena. The Swedish artist Erik Lindberg's portrait was an original representation of Pallas Athena, traditionally depicted in warrior guise with a helmet.

▲ Greta Johansson in full flight. She won gold in the 10 metres women's diving event.

▶ A commemorative plate showing the Stockholm Olympic Stadium. Built by Torben Grut in a style inspired by the palaces of the 16th century, the Stadium underwent a series of transformations during the Games. At one moment it was used for a choral festival and the next a restaurant, but always returning to competition readiness for the following day.

▶▶ Front and back of Olympic dinner menu detailing the food and evening's entertainment autographed by the Prince of Sweden, Gustaf Adolf.

Among the many firsts at the Games in Stockholm were chalked lanes on the athletic track, specialized measuring devices for the bars in high jump and pole vault, and semi-automatic timing and photo-finish equipment. The first official poster was also seen at Stockholm. Designed by Olle Hjortzberg in the Art Nouveau style which was popular at the start of the twentieth century, the poster was translated into 16 languages and used internationally to publicize the Games.

The official programme of events decided upon for Stockholm also included several additions such as the introduction of both pentathlon and decathlon events in athletics and two suggestions of Coubertin's. The first of these suggestions was the sport of modern pentathlon, an event of Coubertin's own creation which combined one sub-event each in fencing, shooting, swimming, riding and running. As part of Coubertin's philosophy that the Olympic Games be about more than just sport, his second suggestion of an art competition was also included.

These additions to the programme would prove to be of note as Coubertin won the gold medal in the literature competition for his 'Ode To Sport' which he entered under the pseudonyms Georges Hohrod and M. Eschbach. Jim Thorpe's athletic prowess led to victories in both the pentathlon and the decathlon.

Thorpe, a tall powerful American, collected his first gold by leading the competition in four of the five sub-events in the pentathlon. He returned the next day to place fourth in the individual high jump and later seventh in the long jump, before winning a second gold in the decathlon in which he was the top performer in six of the 10 sub-events. His world record score would have still won him a silver medal at the 1948 Games.

32

▼◢ The decathlon gold medallist Jim Thorpe in action in several of the event's disciplines.

JIM THORPE (UNITED STATES)

A man of Native American, Irish and French descent whose mother named him Wa-Tho-Huck (Bright Path) he first tried athletics in 1907 when he spotted a high jump contest, joined in and set a school record.

His early renown was as a college American footballer. His small government-run Native American school beat Harvard, with Thorpe scoring all of his school's points, and he was twice chosen as half-back in the All-American college selection.

After Stockholm, he turned to professional baseball with the New York Giants and the Cincinnati Reds, while also playing professional football. In a poll of sportswriters by Associated Press, he was chosen as the greatest athlete of the first half of the 20th century.

"You are the greatest athlete in the world," King Gustav V told him when he presented him with a bronze bust of himself. 'Thanks, King,' Thorpe is reported to have replied. Six months later, after a US newspaper revealed he had been paid $25 a week when he played a season of minor-league baseball, he was disqualified, stripped of both titles and told to return the bronze bust to the IOC. In 1982, the IOC reversed its decision, and replica medals were subsequently awarded to surviving members of his family.

Thorpe's superb performances were matched on the track where a Finn, Hannes Kolehmainen, won three golds and one silver medal and set one world record. Most remarkable of these performances was his run in the 5,000 metres final in which he disputed the lead throughout with a Frenchman, Jean Bouin, edging into the lead only in the final 20 metres and winning by a tenth of a second in a world record of 14:36.6. No man had previously bettered 15 minutes.

▲ First place winner's medal. The obverse is the same as the one designed by Bertram MacKennal for the 1908 Games. The reverse created by Erik Lindberg shows a herald proclaiming the Opening of the Games with, on the left, the statue of Per Henrik Ling, the founder of the institutions and the Swedish gym system.

▲ A sports version of 'Snakes & Ladders' specially produced for the Games, which represents the growing public interest in the Olympics.

▼ The victorious Great Britain 4 x 100 metres freestyle team consisting of Belle Moore, Jennie Fletcher, Annie Speirs and Irene Steer.

34

Philip Noel-Baker, competitor in the 1,500m in 1912, silver medallist in the same event in 1920 and a winner of the Nobel Prize for Peace, said later of the atmosphere of Olympism in Stockholm: "We went to Stockholm as British athletes; we came home Olympians, disciples of the leader, Coubertin, with a new vision I never lost."

Noel-Baker's British team-mate, Arnold Jackson, pulled off a remarkable upset in the 1,500 metres. The field featured the defending champion, Melvin Sheppard, world record holder Abel Kiviat and the one mile world record holder, John Paul Jones, all Americans. Just when an American clean-sweep seemed likely, Jackson edged ahead to win by a mere tenth of a second in an Olympic record time of 3:56.8.

Among other great champions who graced these Games was the Hawaiian swimmer, Duke Paoa Kahanamoku, so named because of a visit to the islands at the time of his father's birth by Queen Victoria's son, the Duke of Edinburgh. He won the 100 metres freestyle by almost two seconds, and collected a silver medal as part of the USA 4 x 200 metres freestyle relay team. Before appearing in minor roles in 28 Hollywood movies he would first compete in three more editions of the Games, winning two more golds and another silver medal.

One oddity of the Games was the longest wrestling bout in its history, an 11-hour 40-minute semi-final in which Martin Klein, of Russia, beat Alfred Asikainen, of Finland. So exhausted was Klein that he could not contest the final, and a Swede Claes Johansson won by default. Another epic was the longest cycle race in Olympic history, a 320 kilometres race that lasted over 10 and a half hours.

◥ The Finn Hannes Kolehmainen raises his hands in triumph as he wins the 10,000 metres.

◀ Russia's Klein finally overcame the Finn, Asiklainen, after an 11-hour wrestling semi-final. So exhausted was Klein, he was unable to contest the final

HANNES KOLEHMAINEN (FINLAND)

The first of a line of great Finnish runners known as the 'Flying Finns' who were to dominate endurance events for nearly 70 years, Kolehmainen, a vegetarian who worked as a bricklayer, came from an athletic family. Both brothers also ran, one becoming the first in 1912 to run a marathon in less than two and a half hours.

After winning golds in the 5,000 and 10,000 metres and the individual cross-country race along with a silver in the cross-country team race in 1912 in Stockholm, Kolehmainen emigrated to New York. He returned eight years later to run for Finland again in the 1920 Games in Antwerp where he won the marathon. He died in 1966, aged 76.

  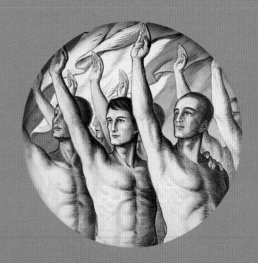

CHAPTER 2

SHAPING THE GAMES

The 1920s and 1930s were a period when the Games took on a more consistent shape. Protocol elements such as the Olympic flag, athletes' oath and Olympic torch relay were all introduced. The programme of sports was defined and streamlined while at the same time it grew as women's participation in the Games increased. More and more of the world's athletes came to participate, with the feats of these new legends creating memorable historic moments.

ANTWERP 1920

On short notice, Antwerp successfully played host to the continuation of the Olympic Games, and athletes from around the world came together to compete in sporting competitions and celebrate the return of peace.

VII OLYMPIAD

Opening date: 20 April 1920

Closing date: 12 September 1920

Country of host city: Belgium (BEL)

Candidate cities: Amsterdam (NED) and Lyon (FRA), who withdrew before the vote

Nations: 29

Events: 154

◀ Official poster designed by Walter Von der Ven and Martha Van Kuyck. It represents the flags of the participating nations all flying together and the coat of arms of the host city. In the centre, the discus thrower is a reference to the Games of Antiquity. The city of Antwerp with the Tower of Notre Dame can be seen in the background.

▼ The first page of a letter from Coubertin to IOC member Godefroy de Blonay announcing his opinion as per the participation of Germany in the Antwerp Games.

38

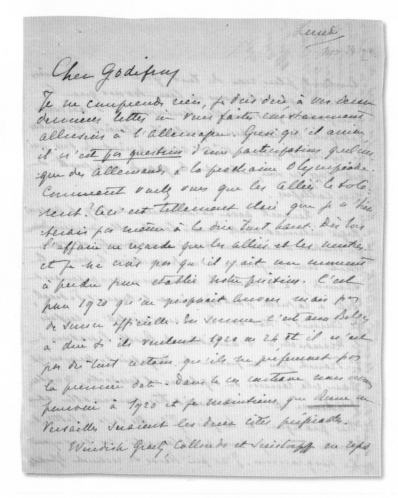

The decision of the International Olympic Committee to designate Antwerp as the host city for the Games of the VII Olympiad not only served to bring together the world's athletes but also to honour the Belgian people for the suffering they had endured during the First World War. With only a short period of time between being given this honour and the opening of the Games, the organizers rapidly made preparations for the celebration, including the building of a 30,000 seat-capacity Olympic Stadium, new pools and sports halls. The short preparation time also proved to be of little consequence to the participants as a then record number of 2,626 athletes came from countries as far away as New Zealand and Argentina to compete and achieve a number of notable performances at the Games.

The celebration got off to a historic start as it was the first at which the official Olympic flag, with its five-ringed Olympic symbol that is representative of the union of the five continents and the colours found in the flags of the nations, flew at the Games. It was also the first time there was a symbolic release of doves at the Opening Ceremony.

Further Olympic history was made during the Opening Ceremony with one more first when the Belgian fencer, swimmer and water polo player, Victor Boin, took the Olympic oath. Boin is most often mentioned for this Olympic first but he is also one of only a small number of Olympic athletes to have participated in more than one sport and win medals in them. He participated in three editions of the Games starting in 1908 in swimming and

▶ Suzanne Lenglen was to become one of the stars of the Games, winning two golds in the tennis events.

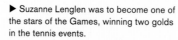

▲ First place winner's medal designed by Josué Dupon. On the obverse, a naked athlete holds a palm leaf and a laurel crown, symbols of victory. Behind him, the figure of the Renommée plays the trumpet.

▶ Belgian athlete Victor Boin takes the Olympic oath on behalf of all athletes during the Opening Ceremony.

PAAVO NURMI (FINLAND)

One of 12 children whose great stamina was founded on early work as an errand boy, he became the greatest runner of the first half of the 20th century. He won every honour available to him, winning nine gold medals and three silvers at three editions of the Olympic Games and setting 22 official world records and 13 at distances not recognized by the sport's world governing body.

His first world record came in 1921; his last in 1931. Many believe he would have been a contender at a fourth Games had he not been declared a professional in 1931 for payments he had received. A copy of a statue of him by Wäinö Aaltonen stands outside Helsinki's Olympic Stadium where he carried the torch at the Opening Ceremony of the 1952 Games.

water polo, where he won a silver, and then switching in 1912 to fencing and water polo, where he won a second medal, a bronze. In 1920 he participated only in fencing and added a silver in the team épée event to his collection.

On the track, not even the impact of the persistent rain could stop newcomer Paavo Nurmi. Following the example set by his Finnish compatriot Hannes Kolehmainen in 1912, Nurmi began compiling an illustrious Olympic record that would span three Games and earn him a total of 12 medals. It all started with the 5,000 metres in Antwerp where he finished 4.4 seconds behind the Frenchman Joseph Guillemot to win a silver medal. He would also take home three golds from these Games, winning the 10,000 metres, the individual 8 kilometres cross country title as well as contributing to the Finnish victory in the team race for this event.

In other displays of running prowess, Hannes Kolehmainen, continued to expand his collection of Olympic medals, winning a gold in the marathon, and Albert Hill, a 31-year-old railway guard from Great Britain, won gold medals in the 800 and 1,500 metres as well as a silver medal in the 3,000 metre team race. Hill's double was a remarkable feat that would not be repeated at an Olympic Games until 44 years later when Peter Snell of New Zealand duplicated the same victorious combination in Tokyo.

◀ The Hawaiian, Duke Kahanamoku, who was nicknamed by the press the 'Human Fish', triumphed in the 100 metres freestyle and 4 x 200 metres freestyle.

▲ The Belgian King dressed in uniform hands out special awards at the Games.

▼ Addressed to Pierre de Coubertin, this invite displays the Olympic rings, which first appeared on IOC documentation in 1913.

DUKE KAHANAMOKU (UNITED STATES)

Of royal blood and born in a royal palace, the Hawaiian's prodigious swimming ability was first noted when he bettered the world best time for 100 yards by five seconds in the open sea in 1911. He went on to win three gold and two silver medals at three editions of the Olympic Games and set seven world records at 100 yards or metres.

Some of Kahanamoku's success came from his use of a 'flutter' kick he had developed to propel his surfboard, and he later went on tours of Australia and the United States to popularize his island's native sport. His Olympic fame also led to appearances in several Hollywood movies.

▶ This rail card allowed Nedo Nadi to travel freely on Italian railways.

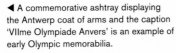

◄ A commemorative ashtray displaying the Antwerp coat of arms and the caption 'VIIme Olympiade Anvers' is an example of early Olympic memorabilia.

► Albert Hill, winner of the 800 metres and 1,500 metres.

▼ The Italian Nedo Nadi's performance was as close to perfection as a fencer could get with him winning three golds in each of the three weapons at one Games.

Popular French tennis player, Suzanne Lenglen, made short work of the competition in the women's singles tennis tournament losing only four games on her way to Olympic gold. Lenglen also partnered with veteran tennis Olympian Max Décugis to win gold in the mixed doubles event and with Elisabeth d'Ayen to take home a third medal, a bronze, in the women's doubles event.

Among other multiple medalists of note were American shooters Willis Lee, with five golds, one silver and one bronze, and Lloyd Spooner with four golds, one silver and two bronzes. Nedo Nadi, of Italy, won five golds with his strong performances in the fencing events, and there were three gold medals each for American swimmers Norman Ross and Ethelda Bleibtrey, a childhood polio victim who won all her events in world record times. In an unusual twist double gold medalist Duke Kahanamoku had to go back in the pool and win his gold medal in the men's 100 metres freestyle a second time after a dispute in the final resulted in the race having to be re-swum.

▼ An Olympic programme showing the Games' Opening Ceremony.

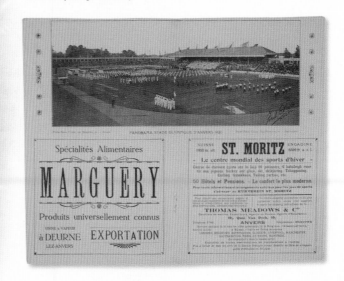

PARIS 1924

The Games returned to Coubertin's native city and for the last time as President of the IOC he witnessed a large jump in the number of competing nations and the increased interest of the media to cover the event, including the first radio broadcast of the Games.

◀ The official Olympic Games poster showing athletes giving the Olympic salute which was derived from the Roman salute.

VIII OLYMPIAD

Opening date: 4 May 1924
Closing date: 27 July 1924
Country of host: France (FRA)
Candidate cities: Amsterdam (NED), Barcelona (ESP), Los Angeles (USA), Prague (CZE), Rome (ITA)
Nations: 44
Events: 126

In 1924, for the first time in the then relatively short history of the modern Olympic Movement, the Games returned to a city that had previously hosted the celebration. The choice of Paris was of special interest to their founder, Pierre de Coubertin, as 1924 marked the 30th anniversary of the decision to revive the Games in a modern form as well as Coubertin's focus on the fact that he would relinquish the IOC presidency a year later.

This edition of the Games, and in particular certain athletics events, would also later serve as the combined factual and fictitious foundation for the Academy award winning movie *Chariots of Fire*. The movie highlighted the actual performances of sprinters Eric Liddell and Harold Abrahams who represented Great Britain at the Games. Unlike the movie, however, Liddell

▲ The Olympic Motto 'Citius, Altius, Fortius' is depicted on this medal. On the reverse is the Olympic salute. It is one of the earliest examples of the Motto being used on Games memorabilia.

▶ Baron Coubertin (front left) with the Prince of Wales. This would be the last Games that Coubertin would attend as IOC President.

knew well in advance of being en route to Paris that the schedule would include competition on Sunday for the 100 metres. Since he also knew that due to his devout Christian beliefs he would not compete in the 100 metres, he was already focused on racing in the 200 and 400 metres events and he did not take the place of his compatriot, Lord David Burghley, in the 400 metres event.

In the real rather than the cinematic version of Olympic competition, the efforts of these two sprinters proved to be just as compelling with Liddell dramatically winning the 400 metres in an Olympic record of 47.6 seconds as well as also gaining a bronze medal in the 200 metres. Against stiff competition from Arthur Porritt of New Zealand, Jackson Scholz and defending Olympic champion Charles Paddock, both from the United States, Abrahams captured the gold in the 100 metres. With his victory Abrahams became the first European to win this Olympic title, equaling the Olympic record of 10.6 seconds three times along the way.

Athletics competitions both on the track and in the long jump pit would add to the memorable sporting moments of these Games. Paavo Nurmi, nicknamed 'The Flying Finn', continued to demonstrate his physical endurance and swift feet in the distance events, undertaking a grueling competition schedule that in no way stopped him from adding five more gold medals to the already impressive collection he had won in 1920. This

◤ The official programme for the season of artistic events held alongside the 1924 Games at the Theatre des Champs-Élysées.

▼ A press entrance ticket for the marathon. The race would be won by Albin Stenroos of Finland.

▼ The obverse of André Rivaud's gold medal design shows the image of a victorious athlete offering a hand to his rival.

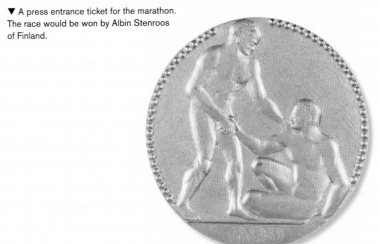

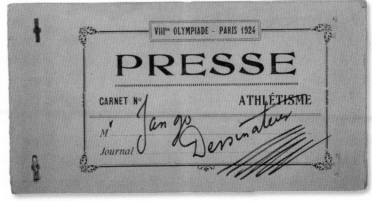

time Nurmi would triumph in the 1,500 metres, 5,000 metres and individual cross country races as well with his team-mates in the 3,000 metres race and the team cross country competition.

Equally impressive in the distance events and clearly possessing a swift set of feet of his own was fellow Finn, Ville Ritola. The efforts of this talented athlete garnered him a total of four gold and two silver medals in 1924 and another gold and silver in 1928. In Paris, Ritola won the 3,000 metres steeplechase and the 10,000 metres, where he broke the world record. He gained silver medals in the 5,000 metres and individual cross country race and then, along with Nurmi, as a member of the Finnish 3,000 metres and cross country teams he won two more golds.

Excellence in the long jump was achieved in a different way by two American athletes. In the case of William DeHart Hubbard, his victory in the actual long jump event also marked the first time that an African American had won an individual Olympic gold in this event. In the pentathlon competition it was another American, Robert LeGendre, who turned in a notable world record breaking long jump performance on his way to a bronze medal.

The aquatics competitions were highlighted by both the introduction of lane dividers in the swimming competitions as well as the performance of American competitor Johnny Weissmuller. Competing in swimming as well as water polo he took away three golds in the 100 metres, 400 metres and 4 x 200 metres freestyle relay events and a bronze as a member of the American water polo team. He would win two more golds in the freestyle competitions in 1928.

▲ William DeHart Hubbard became the first African American to a win gold when he triumphed in the long jump.

▼ Through vigorous training, Harold Abrahams perfected his start, stride and form, which helped him set a new world record and win Olympic gold in the 100 metres.

44

HAROLD ABRAHAMS (GREAT BRITAIN)

The youngest of six children, Abrahams had been motivated as an athlete by elder brother Sidney, a long jumper at the 1912 Games. Harold was himself selected for the event in 1924 after setting an English record but he asked to be excused and instead participated in Paris in the sprints, winning the 100 metres and also taking home a silver medal in the 4 x 100 metres relay.

Ironically, it was an injury while long jumping the following year that ended his running career. Abrahams, however, remained active in sport as a writer, broadcaster and sports administrator.

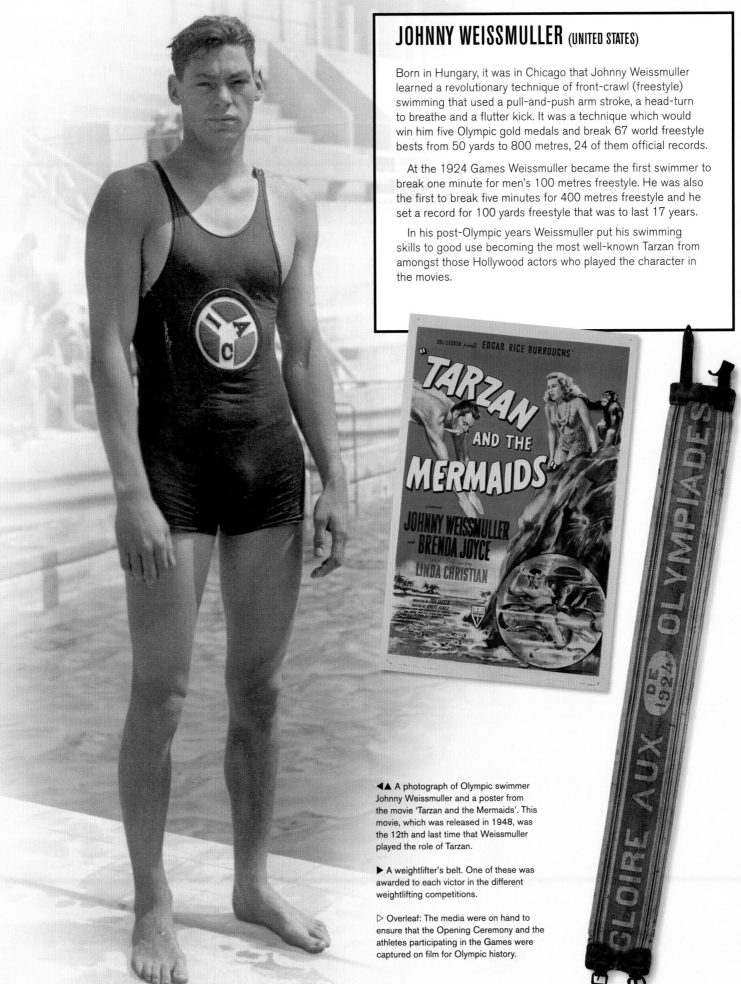

JOHNNY WEISSMULLER (UNITED STATES)

Born in Hungary, it was in Chicago that Johnny Weissmuller learned a revolutionary technique of front-crawl (freestyle) swimming that used a pull-and-push arm stroke, a head-turn to breathe and a flutter kick. It was a technique which would win him five Olympic gold medals and break 67 world freestyle bests from 50 yards to 800 metres, 24 of them official records.

At the 1924 Games Weissmuller became the first swimmer to break one minute for men's 100 metres freestyle. He was also the first to break five minutes for 400 metres freestyle and he set a record for 100 yards freestyle that was to last 17 years.

In his post-Olympic years Weissmuller put his swimming skills to good use becoming the most well-known Tarzan from amongst those Hollywood actors who played the character in the movies.

◀▲ A photograph of Olympic swimmer Johnny Weissmuller and a poster from the movie 'Tarzan and the Mermaids'. This movie, which was released in 1948, was the 12th and last time that Weissmuller played the role of Tarzan.

▶ A weightlifter's belt. One of these was awarded to each victor in the different weightlifting competitions.

▷ Overleaf: The media were on hand to ensure that the Opening Ceremony and the athletes participating in the Games were captured on film for Olympic history.

AMSTERDAM 1928

A symbolic fire was lit for the first time and a change to the order of the parade of nations during the Opening Ceremony led to the start of a new Olympic tradition.

◀ A German-language graphic for the 1928 Games, featuring a classically styled athlete and the Dutch flag.

▼ An entrance ticket for the Opening Ceremony where a symbolic fire was lit for the first time.

IX OLYMPIAD

Opening date: 17 May 1928
Closing date: 12 August 1928
Country of host city: Netherlands (NED)
Candidate city: Los Angeles (USA)
Nations: 46
Events: 109

Surrounded by the backdrop of architect Jan Wils' Olympic stadium, spectators at the Opening Ceremony welcomed the world's athletes. Competitors from around the globe paraded into the stadium in alphabetical order by nation, with two exceptions. In homage to the ancient Olympic connection, the Games organizers had decided that the Greek team would lead the parade and the host Dutch team would enter last. It proved to be the start of a new Olympic tradition.

Just outside the stadium, the precursor of another Olympic tradition was kindled when a symbolic flame was lit for the first time. Its location was atop the marathon tower. The tower, along with the stadium and several of the competition venues, was designed by Jan Wils to meet the Organizing Committee's wish, and Pierre de Coubertin's dream, to realize the idea of an 'Olympic City'. Wils's contribution towards turning this idea into the reality led him to receive a medal of his own. His design for the Olympic Stadium earned him the gold in the architecture category of the Olympic arts competitions.

48

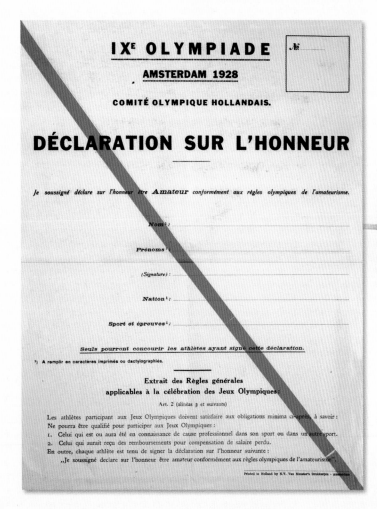

◀ The 1928 Summer Olympics was the first Games in which female athletes competed in athletics events. Canadian Ethel Catherwood became the first woman's high jump champion, clearing 1.59 metres.

▼ An ornate Art Deco diploma of merit awarded to the incoming IOC President Henri de Baillet-Latour by the Dutch National Organizing Committee.

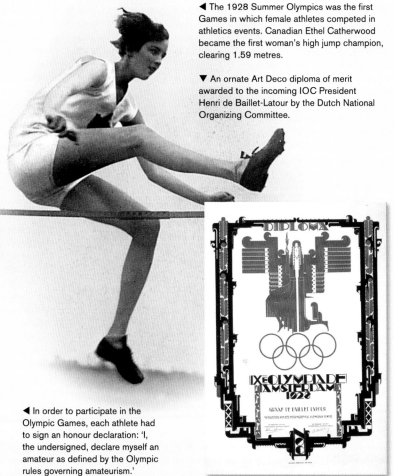

◀ In order to participate in the Olympic Games, each athlete had to sign an honour declaration: 'I, the undersigned, declare myself an amateur as defined by the Olympic rules governing amateurism.'

For the sports competitions, changes to the Olympic programme and participation figures were influenced by women, the definition of an amateur, and the entry of new nations. Tennis was eliminated from the programme due to debate over payments for loss of earnings to its athletes. The number of events for women increased with the introduction of a women's team gymnastics event and five athletics competitions. Hand in hand with this, the number of female Olympic participants more than doubled. Athletes from Rhodesia and Panama competed for the first time.

In the women's high jump competition Canadian Ethel Catherwood demonstrated that a woman could be feminine and athletically successful. Dubbed the 'Saskatoon Lily' by the media, in reference to where she lived and her good looks, Catherwood not only won the gold medal but also set a world record in the semi-final of the event. Unfortunately, performances in the women's 800 metres race did not prove to be as promising. Despite a world record finish by gold medalist Karoline 'Lina' Radke of Germany, the collapse of several of the women following the completion of the event led to its elimination from the Olympic programme for the next 32 years.

The men's athletics competitions were notable for providing several surprise performances. The first came about thanks to Canadian Percy Williams, a relative unknown outside his native Vancouver until he won the national trials in 1928. Even still, at the Games he did the unexpected, equaling the men's 100 metres Olympic record of 10.6 seconds in the second round of the competition before going on to win the gold in the event and pick up another gold for his win in the 200 metres. Another surprise

PERCY WILLIAMS (CANADA)

Percy Williams, the winner of Canada's first 100 metres gold, was an unlikely sporting hero. He suffered rheumatic fever in his teens and doctors said he should never overexert himself again but two years later, encouraged by his school headmaster in Vancouver, he raced a local champion and the result was a tie.

That started him running at 18 and, trained carefully by a sympathetic coach, he won his first national title and became the double Olympic sprint champion in 1928. An injured thigh muscle would ultimately prevent Williams from defending his titles in 1932 and effectively put an end to his running career.

49

▲ This glass is an example of some of the souvenirs produced for the Games which were inspired by stylistic Art Deco designs.

▶ Canadian Percy Williams is carried in celebration following his victory in the 100 metres sprint.

▼ Wooden clogs signed by the US Olympic team.

was the victory of Britain's Douglas Lowe in the 800 metres, after a German, Otto Peltzer, who had beaten Lowe in a world record time two years earlier, was eliminated by injury in the semi-finals. Both Williams and Lowe would later prove that their Olympic performances had not merely been a case of luck as Williams set a world record in the 100 metres in 1930 and Lowe won an unofficial rematch against Peltzer shortly after the Games.

In the other competition venues there were a number of equally notable performances. Youth had its way in the swimming pool when Albina Osipowich, an American, won golds in the 100 metres and 4 x 100 metres relay at just 17. In yachting, Crown Prince Olav of Norway won a gold in the six metres class, becoming the first of four future kings to compete at the Olympic Games. In hockey, India began what would become a six Games gold medal winning streak.

Medal winning performances were matched by examples of fair play and gentlemanly behaviour to both ducks and fellow athletes. Australian Henry Pearce stopped rowing during his quarter final race in order to allow a family of ducks to pass in front of his boat. Nonetheless, he still managed to win the race and go on to also win the gold medal in the final of the event. In a heat of the 3,000 metres steeplechase race, Paavo Nurmi took a tumble head first into the water on one of the jumps but was graciously helped out by Frenchman Lucien Duquesne.

◀ Medal designed by Giuseppe Cassioli. It was selected after an IOC competition. On the obverse, a Victory figure is holding a palm in her left hand and a winner's crown in her right. This design was used on the obverse of Olympic Summer Games medals until 2000.

▼ Yoshiyuki Tsuruta, winner of the gold medal in 200 metres breaststroke, shaking the hand of a compatriot.

LORD DAVID BURGHLEY (GREAT BRITAIN)

David Burghley, heir to the Marquess of Exeter, a title he was to inherit in 1956, competed as an athlete at three Olympic Games, winning the 400 metres hurdles in an Olympic record time of 53.4 in 1928 and a silver in the 4 x 400 metres relay four years later in Los Angeles in 1932.

A year after his final Games he became a member of the IOC. He was later president of the International Amateur Athletic Federation and chaired the Organizing Committee of the 1948 Games of the XIV Olympiad in London. His non-sporting positions included being elected a British Member of Parliament and the Governor of Bermuda.

▲ Cover of a musical score. The graphics use strong lines, bold color scheme and reflect the Art Deco style. The second flag is that of the city of Amsterdam.

▲ Two Finns, Viho Ritola and Paavo Nurmi, battle it out in the 10,000 metres. Nurmi would be the eventual victor.

▶ Competing for France, Boughera Mohamed El Ouafi won the Olympic gold in the marathon.

◢ This toffee box was produced for the Amsterdam Games by the Van Melle firm. The company paid great attention to packaging and the use of the colour orange by them matched its use on many other Games related items.

LOS ANGELES 1932

The Games took place Hollywood-style in 1932 and for a short time the magic of the Olympic Games permitted people to leave behind the Great Depression and instead marvel at the feats of many talented athletes.

◀ Official poster by Julio Kilenyi. This poster takes its inspiration from the ancient Olympic Games custom of sending messengers to announce the dates of the next celebration of the Games and proclaim the sacred truce.

◤ The gold medal design remained identical to the 1928 Games with only the date and host city changing.

X OLYMPIAD

Opening date: 30 July 1932
Closing date: 14 August 1932
Country of host city: United States (USA)
Candidate cities: None
Nations: 37
Events: 117

▶▶ Silver-coloured metal bracelet. The design is inspired by Native American artwork, the five-ring Olympic symbol and the Olympic Motto 'Citius, Altius, Fortius'.

▶ 'Eddie' Tolan stands on the podium prior to receiving one of his gold medals.

52

Originally awarded to Los Angeles in 1923, the subsequent Great Depression that resulted from the crash of the U.S. stock market in 1929 did little to put a damper on the Games of the X Olympiad. Instead, innovative planning, remarkable performances and a touch of Hollywood glamour were the rule of the day when athletes from 37 nations came together in the summer of 1932.

When it came to planning for the celebration of the Games and attracting athletes from around the world to take part, the Organizing Committee knew it had a challenge to face. Their solutions, however, proved to be tempting enough. Not only did they persuade rail companies and steamship lines to give national teams cheaper fares, but they also managed to reduce the cost of food and housing for the athletes by erecting the first official Olympic Village.

The idea of building an Olympic Village for the male athletes in Los Angeles was motivated by much more than a desire to merely minimize costs. A place where the athletes' comfort and health

THOMAS 'EDDIE' TOLAN (UNITED STATES)

At just 1.70 metres, Thomas 'Eddie' Tolan, dubbed 'the Midnight Express', is the shortest man ever to have won the Olympic 100 metres. Neither his height, which ended his dream of becoming a football player, nor the bandage he had to wear round his left knee due to an injury, hindered his Olympic performance.

The man from Detroit twice equalled the world record of 10.4 seconds in 1929, when only 20, and beat it in 1930 with 10.2, a record never officially ratified because of the absence of a wind gauge. He failed to win the 1932 US Olympic trial but at the Games he would just edge out Ralph Metcalfe, in the 100 metres, equalling the world record of 10.3 seconds that had been set by Percy Williams in 1930. Tolan also raced to another victory in the 200 metres.

could be guaranteed, it was also a setting in which organizers also hoped that the participants could come together to mix and mingle, relax and get to know each other. It is evident from the team reports and newspaper coverage during the Games that the Village was a success, proving to be equally as memorable for the public due to the athletes it housed as it was for the athletes themselves who enjoyed the hospitality provided there.

Performances in the competition venues also led to memorable moments and the emergence of more than a few sporting luminaries who easily gave the stars of Hollywood a run for their money. While 'America's Sweetheart', Mary Pickford, and her swashbuckler husband, Douglas Fairbanks, were livening up the social side of the Games, athletes such as Mildred 'Babe' Didrikson and Juan Carlos Zabala were providing entertainment of their own.

A talented all-around athlete who excelled at basketball, golf and athletics, the American Babe Didrikson took advantage of the addition of two new women's events in the athletics competition, collecting gold in both. She won the javelin competition with

▶ Representing Austria, Ellen Preis won the women's individual foil fencing competition. She would compete in four other editions of the Games and win two more medals, both bronze.

◣ The Argentinian Juan Carlos Zabala exhausted after narrowly winning the marathon.

53

a record setting throw on her first attempt and the 80 metres hurdles with another record setting performance of 11.7 seconds. In an extremely tight high jump competition that required a jump-off, both Didrikson and her team-mate Jean Shiley set a new world record. It was Shiley, however, who ultimately came away with the gold and Didrikson the silver after one judge ruled Babe's western-roll technique illegal.

Despite the exclusion of Paavo Nurmi on the grounds of professionalism, the marathon proved to be a memorable event. In a dramatic finish, that was so close that the first four runners were in the stadium for the final lap of the track at the same time, the young Argentinian Juan Carlos Zabala managed to hold on long enough to claim the title of Olympic champion. For the second place finisher, Samuel Ferris of Great Britain, it would be his third and last Olympic appearance and his best result at the Games.

MILDRED 'BABE' DIDRIKSON (UNITED STATES)

This Texan typist was an all-round sporting talent. An All-American at high school basketball, she took part in eight of the ten events at the 1932 US Olympic trials and won six. At the Olympics, the rules prevented her taking part in more than three events, but the limitation did not prevent her from winning medals in all three.

Later in life, she became an outstanding golfer and was voted the greatest female athlete of the half-century in 1950. She won 14 straight golf tournaments in one 12-month period along with the British Amateur Open. After surgery for cancer she returned to win the US Open by 12 strokes. She died at the age of 45 in 1956.

54

▲ Lauri Lehtinen claimed victory in the hotly contested 5,000 metres race.

◀ To add to her javelin success Mildred Didrikson broke another Olympic record and won gold in the women's 80 metres hurdles.

Drama Hollywood style continued to be the theme of the athletic events as fierce competition tactics on the part of eventual gold medalist Lauri Lehtinen of Finland took the place of fair play on the track during the running of the 5,000 metres. Fortunately, more positive examples of competitive spirit as well as examples of sporting excellence were to be found in other venues and in other sports contests though.

In the fencing competitions, Austrian competitor Ellen Preis reaped the benefit of the kindness of her opponent Heather 'Judy' Guinness in the women's individual foil competition. Thanks to the fact that Guinness pointed out to officials that they had neglected to count two touches that Preis had scored against her, Preis was awarded the victory and the gold and Guinness the silver.

At the cinema, former Olympic swimming medalist turned Hollywood movie actor Johnny Weissmuller was creating a splash with the premier of his first *Tarzan* movie. Meanwhile, a contingent of Japanese athletes were making waves with strong performances throughout in the mens' events. The winner of the 1,500 metres freestyle, Kusuo Kitamura, aged 14, became the youngest known male athlete in an individual event to win a medal.

◀ A miniature village was created by the Standard Paper Box Corporation at the request of Paul Helms, who provided the bread for the Village. It consisted of various buildings and although not true replicas, one piece was offered with every Helms Bakery product bought.

◥ A key for the Olympic Village consisting of a number of small portable 'Olympic cottages', which was built for the male athletes. The women were housed separately in the Chapman Park Hotel.

BERLIN 1936

The Games got off to a memorable start with the introduction of the Olympic torch relay and the momentum continued to build as the athletes and their performances became the stars of the celebration.

XI OLYMPIAD

Opening date: 1 August 1936
Closing date: 16 August 1936
Country of host city: Germany (GER)
Candidate city: Barcelona (ESP)
Nations: 49
Events: 129

◄ Berlin's official poster by Frantz Würbel. It depicted a larger-than-life wreathed champion and the host city's most well known landmark, the quadriga from the Brandenburg Gate.

▼ The first Olympic torch designed by the sculptor Walter Lemcke. The route from Olympia to Berlin was engraved on the handle of the torch. It was produced in polished, stainless steel by the Krupp firm in Essen.

▲ The Olympic torch relay made its first appearance at Berlin. It was carried in relay from Olympia where the Olympic flame was lit to the Games host city of Berlin.

► Letter from the IOC President Baillet-Latour to German sports leaders expressing concerns about the organization of the upcoming Games in Berlin.

Today's association of the 1936 Olympic Games to Jesse Owens and Adolf Hitler and the use by some individuals of the term 'Nazi Olympics' to describe the event would have been impossible to predict when the IOC designated Berlin as the host city in 1931. In point of fact, when Berlin was selected as Olympic host, Jesse Owens was not yet a rising star in athletics and Adolf Hitler's National Socialist Party, the 'Nazi' Party, had yet to be elected.

Nonetheless, in the period between the designation of Berlin and the Opening Ceremony of the Games of the XI Olympiad, times and German politics changed. Calls for a boycott due to the Nazi's anti-Semitic, Aryan superiority way of thinking, however, ultimately had little impact. Support for a boycott was minimal, with only a few countries and some individual athletes choosing not to attend.

Instead, the Olympic Games took place in Berlin as scheduled and an innovative idea and the talents of a number of athletes, and not just Jesse Owens, outshone the politics. While the Aryan imagery on the official poster and the use of the German eagle and the Brandenburg Gate on Olympic souvenirs and artefacts as well as the images of banners with the swastika became a part of the 1936 Olympic history, so too did the remarkable performances of the athletes gathered in Berlin for the Games of the XI Olympiad.

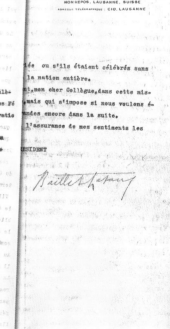

JOHN LOVELOCK (NEW ZEALAND)

John Lovelock's athletic career almost ended before it began because of a serious rugby injury but, recovered, he came to the forefront while he was a Rhodes scholar at Oxford University. His form there earned him a place on the New Zealand team for the 1,500 metres at the 1932 Olympics where he finished ninth. A year later he set his first world record.

He became his country's first Olympic champion in 1936 and then later a qualified doctor. A fall from a horse left him prone to dizzy spells, and he died in 1949 at the age of only 38 after falling in front of a subway train in New York.

▲ The gold medal styling remained true to Guiseppe Cassioli's design for the 1928 Olympic Games.

▶ John Lovelock's victory in the 1,500 metres was a first Olympic gold won by an athlete representing New Zealand.

▼ Leather change purse. For 1936, most souvenirs made for the Games incorporated the Olympic rings and an image of the 13.809 kg bell that was specially cast for the Games in Berlin. The bell was decorated with the German eagle designed by Johannes Boehland and the phrase 'Ich rufe die Jugend der Welt' or 'I summon the youth of the world' was engraved around it.

Jesse Owens became a star of the Games both on and off the track. He took away Olympic gold in the men's 100 and 200 metres, the long jump and in the 4 x 100 metres relay. He also became known for the friendship that developed between him and German long jumper 'Luz' Long.

Other impressive performances were turned in by athletes on and in the water as well as on the track and the polo field.

Competing in his fifth Olympic Games, Jack Beresford of Great Britain took home his fifth medal in the rowing competitions. It was a rowing performance record that would not be beaten until the Games in Sydney in 2000.

In the pool, Hendrika 'Rie' Mastenbroek of the Netherlands won gold in the women's 100 and 400 metres freestyle events as well as in the 4 x 100 metres freestyle relay, all in Olympic record time. She also won a silver in the 100 metres backstroke. American Marjorie Gestring dove her way to a gold in the women's springboard event and in doing so became the youngest ever female gold medalist in the event at the age of 13 years 268 days. Meanwhile, Inge Sörensen became the youngest female to win a medal of any colour in an event when she earned a bronze in the women's 200 metres breaststroke at the age of 12 years and 24 days.

The men's 1,500 metres turned into a highly competitive final as New Zealander John Lovelock outran American Glenn Cunningham for the gold. Both beat the world record and the three competitors behind them all surpassed the Olympic record.

In other sports, canoeing and basketball joined the programme for the first time and polo made its last appearance at the Games with a strong performance by the team from Argentina. It was a performance that led them to gold and the distinction of being the last Olympic champions in the sport.

For the first time at an Olympic celebration the people in the host city had the opportunity to witness all of these spectacular performances without actually having to have a ticket. Instead,

▲ The Olympic salute was derived from the Roman salute but because of its similarity to the Nazi salute it was abandoned in 1947.

▶ Jesse Owens's achievements are the enduring memory of the Games in Berlin. His four golds was the perfect defiance to the Nazi regime.

▼ The 1936 Games included men's basketball and handball for the first time.

◢ Jesse Owens's shoes which he wore on his way to victory in the 100 metres, 200 metres, long jump and 4 x 100 metres relay.

▶ American Marjorie Gestring won the 3 metre springboard diving event at the age of 13 years and 268 days, becoming the youngest woman to win an Olympic gold medal.

◀ Extract from a circular letter sent to all National Olympic Committees to inform them of Olympic Village services, including a questionnaire on teams' dietary requirements.

▷ Overleaf: Partial view of the exterior and interior of the Olympic Stadium.

JESSE OWENS (UNITED STATES)

The youngest of 10 children of an Alabama cotton picker, he was christened James Cleveland. It was a schoolteacher, mishearing him call out his name as J. C. Owens, who created a name that became synonymous with superlative sporting performance.

Owens, himself a cotton picker by the age of seven and a husband and a father by the age of 18, went on to attend Ohio State University. He repaid his benefactors by setting five world records and equalling one at the 1935 NCAA championships. A year later in Berlin he won four Olympic golds before turning professional.

locals were able to follow the Games free of charge as television viewing rooms were set up in the Greater Berlin area to show footage of the dramas that were played out in the sporting arenas, thereby allowing more people than ever to experience the excitement of the Games.

Before the Games had even begun a new Olympic tradition was born, thanks to Carl Diem. Like Coubertin, Diem too found inspiration in ancient Greek examples, although not ones that came from the ancient Olympic Games. Instead, Diem developed his idea from the examples of torch races that had been held at other events during ancient Greek times. The result was the introduction of the first Olympic torch relay.

Lit from the rays of the sun at the site of the ancient Games in Olympia, the Olympic flame was transported by male runners from Olympia to Berlin over a 12-day period of time, travelling through seven countries along the way. Images of the relay were preserved forever in Leni Riefenstahl's now legendary film of the Games, *Olympia*. Additionally, German 1,500 metres runner Fritz Schilgen had his name entered into Olympic history books not as an Olympic medalist or even a competitor but rather as the first individual to light the flame to the Olympic cauldron.

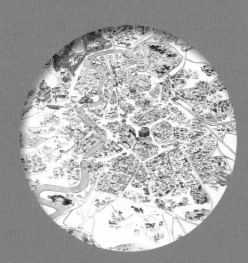

CHAPTER 3

THE GAMES REBOUND

After a 12-year absence, the Games returned, giving London, Helsinki and Tokyo a second chance to host a Games edition that war had prevented. Rome too had a different second chance, while Melbourne became an Olympic first for 'Down Under'. As the world rebounded, so too did the Games, with a widening audience thanks to television, an emphasis on celebrations designed to mix culture with sport, and an expanding Olympic Movement contributing to the event.

LONDON 1948

Following the cancellation of two editions of the Olympic Games in 1940 and 1944, the challenge of staging the Games of the XIV Olympiad amidst post-War shortages was taken up by London.

◀ London's official poster by Walter Herz. It shows the Houses of Parliament and the famous Ancient Greece statue of the 'Discobolus'. The time shows 4 o'clock, the time of the Opening Ceremony.

Originally chosen to host the 1944 Games, which were cancelled due to World War II, London again sought the opportunity when fighting ceased and peace returned. In May 1946 a postal vote by the IOC led to London being chosen again, this time for the Games of the XIV Olympiad to take place in 1948. Despite the fact that the city, as well as the country as a whole, were still recovering from the War, its citizens and the Organizing Committee rose to the challenges presented by shortages of housing, food and equipment.

Many of these challenges were overcome by the use of existing facilities for both sports and accommodation. Henley-on-Thames was used for both the canoeing and rowing events in order to reduce costs. The Empire pool was also used for more than one sport, serving for both aquatics events and then, with a scaffold bridge placed in the water of the pool and a ring placed on top of that, for boxing. The accommodation of the participants was solved by the use of military camps, schools, colleges and hotels.

XIV OLYMPIAD

Opening date: 29 July 1948
Closing date: 14 August 1948
Country of host city: Great Britain (GBR)
Candidate cities: Baltimore (USA), Lausanne (SUI), Los Angeles (USA), Minneapolis (USA), Philadelphia (USA)
Nations: 59
Events: 136

◀ Three types of torches were used for the relay: a standard torch, a torch with a gas recipient for the sea crossing and a torch for the last runner. The standard torch, shown here, was made of stainless steel.

▶ The Czechoslovakian long-distance runner, Emil Zátopek, set new standards for the 10,000 metres, lapping all but two rivals in his run to the gold medal.

EMIL ZÁTOPEK (CZECHOSLOVAKIA)

Emil Zátopek ranks as one of the finest long-distance competitors. His first Olympic title in London only hinted at the success that was to come. He revolutionized endurance running and set a total of eighteen world records in distances ranging from 5,000 metres to 30 kilometres. At the 1952 Olympic Games in Helsinki he also established another record, a unique and to this day unduplicated Olympic triple, winning the 5,000 and 10,000 metres as well as the marathon.

A Czech national hero, his support for a liberal uprising against Communists in 1968 cost him his army rank of colonel and he was reduced to menial jobs for many years but Zátopek would eventually triumph over even this.

◀ American Robert Mathias became the youngest decathlon champion at the age of 17.

▶ Three months after graduating with honours from the French Conservatory of Music, playing the piano, Micheline Ostermeyer used her hands rather less delicately to win gold medals in both the discus and shot-put events.

▼ The Swiss equestrian team finished fourth in the Three-Day Event despite the best efforts of Alfred Blaser and his mount Mahmud.

The question of how to feed all the athletes and officials during a time when there was still rationing demonstrated both flexibility and generosity. Arrangements were made so that each National Olympic Committee had the option to supply their own food. Additionally, countries gave gifts for all the participants such as 100 tons of fresh fruit from the Dutch Olympic Committee and 160,000 eggs from Denmark.

After some debate, the Organizers made the decision to continue with the new tradition of the Olympic torch relay. Lit in Olympia, at the site of the ancient Olympic Games, the flame passed from Olympia through a small number of European countries before arriving in Great Britain. Highlights of this journey included the action of the first runner, Corporal Dimitrelis of the Greek Army, who laid down his gun and took off his uniform to

reveal the clothing of an athlete that he wore underneath. It was a symbolic reference to the truce of the ancient Olympic Games and a memorable beginning to the relay. A link was also made to the modern Olympic Games with a stop at the IOC headquarters and the tomb of Pierre de Coubertin in Lausanne, Switzerland.

Despite the fact that the impact of the War was clearly visible in the planning for the Games there was still a place for innovation, growth in participant numbers and the introduction of new events. Starting blocks were seen for the first time and the starters' pistol was linked to an electronic timer. A greater number of women and countries participated than ever before and several new women's and men's events were added to the sports programme.

Fanny Blankers-Koen of the Netherlands was just one of the athletes to take advantage of the introduction of these new events. She had victories in the 100 metres, 80 metres hurdles and as a member of the Dutch women's 4 x 100 metres relay team as well as in the newly introduced women's 200 metres event for a total of four golds.

Outstanding among the men on the track were Olympic newcomers Emil Zátopek of Czechoslovakia and Robert Mathias of the United States. For Zátopek the 10,000 metres was an easy victory as he lapped all but two runners and crossed the finish line with a lead of more than 300 metres to win in an Olympic record time. In the 5,000 it was a different story as the Belgian runner Gaston Reiff was able to hold off Zátopek and take home the gold

66

▲ The 1948 starters' pistol automatically triggered the electronic timer and was used at the Olympic Games for the first time.

◄ The Dutch housewife and mother of two, Fanny Blankers-Koen, returned to the Games 12 years after competing at Berlin and won four gold medals.

▲ The gold medal design remained unchanged, taking inspiration from the Olympic Games design for Amsterdam 1928.

FANNY BLANKERS-KOEN (NETHERLANDS)

Fanny Blankers competed in Berlin in 1936 at the age of 18 in the women's 4 x 100 metres relay and the high jump. During her athletic career she set a total of 16 world records in eight different events, won five European titles and 58 national titles in the Netherlands.

With such an impressive record it is no surprise that it included four medals at the 1948 Olympic Games in London. Following the Games there she returned home to be given a gift of a bicycle by her neighbours, 'so you won't have to run so much'.

by just a stride. Mathias had only competed in his first decathlon a mere three months prior to the Games. Nonetheless, neither the delays due to poor weather on the second day that stretched the competition to 12 hours in duration nor the fact that the last two events had to be illuminated by car headlights stopped Mathias from becoming the youngest Olympic decathlon champion at just 17 years of age.

The athletes in the decathlon were not the only ones to have to sometimes compete as day turned to night or weather made change necessary. Cycling events at the Herne Hill track in South London finished in the dark and all that could be seen of the riders on the back straight was their white vests. Cyclists and journalists alike adapted to these conditions in creative ways with journalists filing reports to their newspapers in unlit telephone booths using matches or lighters to illuminate their notes. In the case of gymnastics, wet weather and muddy conditions led to a venue change but once again the organizers showed the adaptability that made the Games a success, relocating the competitions to an indoor venue.

▲ Octagonal shaped tray. This tray shows Wembley Stadium and a torch runner. Its style and shape was common to the time period.

▼ For the first time, officials were able to decide close finishes by the use of a camera.

▲ Despite losing his right hand during military training, Károly Takacs was able to shoot left-handed and won the rapid-fire pistol gold medal in both 1948 and four years later.

▶ Commemorative badge showing the Houses of Parliament, Big Ben Tower and the Olympic symbol.

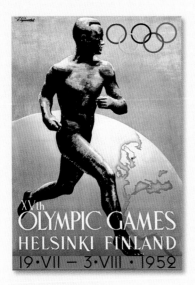

HELSINKI 1952

Although Helsinki was the smallest city to have hosted the Games it did not stop athletes such as Viktor Chukarin, Emil Zátopek, Edoardo Mangiarotti and others from producing big results there.

◀ Official poster designed by Ilmari Sysimetsä. It had been created for the 1940 Games, which were not held due to World War II and shows a bronze statue of Finnish track legend Paavo Nurmi by Wäinö Aaltonen.

XV OLYMPIAD

Opening date: 19 July 1952
Closing date: 3 August 1952
Country of host city: Finland (FIN)
Candidate cities: Amsterdam
  (NED), Chicago (USA),
  Detroit (USA), Los Angeles
  (USA), Minneapolis (USA),
  Philadelphia (USA)
Nations: 69
Events: 149

When the Games of the XV Olympiad for 1952 were awarded to the city of Helsinki it was a second chance for its citizens to realize their unfulfilled dream of hosting the Olympic Games. Their first chance, an offer to host the Olympic Games of 1940, had come about after the Japanese city of Tokyo found itself no longer able to perform the role due to war in their country. Ironically, the same fate awaited Helsinki as the escalating hostilities that led to World War II ultimately made it impossible for the Games of the XII Olympiad to be held in 1940.

For 1952, however, dreams were fulfilled. Facilities that had either been completed or been well on their way to completion for 1940 were given new life and quickly made ready for 1952. The velodrome and swimming stadium that had been under construction in 1940 and later completed at the end of World War II were ready for use well in advance of the 1952 Games. The Olympic Stadium was only slightly modified to increase the spectator seating capacity from approximately 50,000 to 70,000 places and repairs were made to the running track, jumping pits and throwing areas.

◀ Torch designed by the Finnish artist Aukusti Tuhka. Only 22 torches were made and are therefore now very rare. During the Opening Ceremony, Paavo Nurmi carried the torch into the stadium and lit a cauldron at track-level. The torch was then passed to Hannes Kolehmainen who lit another Olympic cauldron at the top of the stadium tower.

◣ Australian Marjorie Jackson dominated the women's sprint events between 1950 and 1954.

MARJORIE JACKSON (AUSTRALIA)

Marjorie Jackson, nicknamed 'the Lithgow Flash', won the women's 100 and 200 metres sprints in Helsinki. Jackson achieved this performance double at both the 1950 and 1954 Empire Games, also winning three relay gold medals along the way. Three times she achieved the sprint double in the Australian championships.

She was undefeated in major competitions and during five sensational years, she broke 18 world records, a tally never since equalled. She retired from the track in 1954, still only 23, when she married Australian Olympic cyclist Peter Nelson.

The first coin issued to commemorate the modern Olympic Games shows a laurel wreath and the Olympic rings. 600,000 coins were issued.

Guide for the camp sites which were specially built to accommodate Olympic guests.

The USSR and Israel attended the Olympic Games for the first time. This diploma was awarded to Soviet gymnast Galina Urbanovitch who won a gold medal in the team competition and a silver in the team portable apparatus event.

One of the stars of Helsinki was Adhemar Ferreira Da Silva. He was the only Brazlian athlete to win gold at the 1952 Games.

One facility that did need some modification though was accommodation. While options such as camp sites were available to spectators at the Games, the organizers for 1952 faced the challenge of looking for housing for the athletes. The Organizing Committee proved they were up to the challenge, however. They built new housing for the male competitors and then made use of several different existing facilities to house the women and even created a separate Village, at the request of the Soviets, for not only the Soviet athletes but also those of other 'Soviet-bloc' countries.

With the planning taken care of, the Games were ready to begin. Before new history could be made though, it was past Olympic history that became a memorable highlight of the Opening Ceremony. Already a tradition, the arrival of the Olympic flame was made all the more special by the organizers' decision to have two final torchbearers and two cauldrons. It would have been next to impossible for them to do otherwise as the two men who were given the honour, Finnish long distance runners Paavo Nurmi and Hannes Kolehmainen, were both equally legendary.

New Olympic history was just as quickly made as the competitions got under way. Part of that new history was again focused on the long distance running as Emil Zátopek did what neither Nurmi nor Kolehmainen had ever done, winning Olympic gold in the 5,000 and 10,000 metres as well as the marathon. For the Zátopek family there was still more gold to be mined as Emil's wife Dana won her own gold medal in the women's javelin event.

The athletics events were also notable for producing a number of surprise results. Josef Barthel of Luxembourg won the 1,500 metres in a race in which future four minute mile record breaker Roger Bannister was placed fourth. Adhemar Ferreira Da Silva of Brazil hopped, stepped and jumped his way to a gold medal with an Olympic and world record performance of 16.22 metres in the triple jump. Meanwhile a contingent of Jamaican athletes put on an impressive performance that included a world and Olympic record breaking gold medal victory in the men's 4 x 400 metres relay.

In shooting, Károly Takács of Hungary, who had lost his right hand in an accident with a grenade, once again proved his versatility as he shot instead with his left and retained the rapid-fire pistol title he won in 1948. Another athlete to score victory by his left hand was Italian fencer Edoardo Mangiarotti. In Helsinki he won golds in the individual and team épée events as well as silvers in the individual and team foil events to add to what would eventually become an impressive Olympic career record, competing in five editions of the Games and collecting a total of 13 Olympic medals.

It was to be expected with a team of roughly 290 athletes that some of the memorable performances would be provided by the athletes of the Soviet Union who were making their first appearance at the Games. In particular, they shone in the women's athletics field events and both the men's and women's gymnastics as athletes such as Aleksandra Chudina, Viktor Chukarin, and Mariya Gorokhovskaya demonstrated just how prepared they were to compete and win.

70

▲ The high point of Emil Zátopek's career came in Helsinki. He wore the shoes shown here during the marathon.

▶ Venues and city map containing basic information on the Olympic programme, tickets prices and transportation.

◀◀ Robert 'Bob' Mathias became the first the athlete to retain the decathlon title, and did so with a record score of 7,887 points.

ROBERT 'BOB' MATHIAS (UNITED STATES)

Two years after winning Olympic gold in London in 1948, Mathias set the first of his three world records. His third record came in Helsinki as he accumulated 7,887 points, won a second Olympic gold and became the first man to defend his Olympic decathlon title.

Mathias won all 11 competitions he took part in – including four US national championships – before being declared professional for appearing in a film about his own sporting career. He later turned to politics, and in 1966 he was elected as a Republican congressman, serving for eight years, and he also later served as the first director of the US Olympic Training Centre.

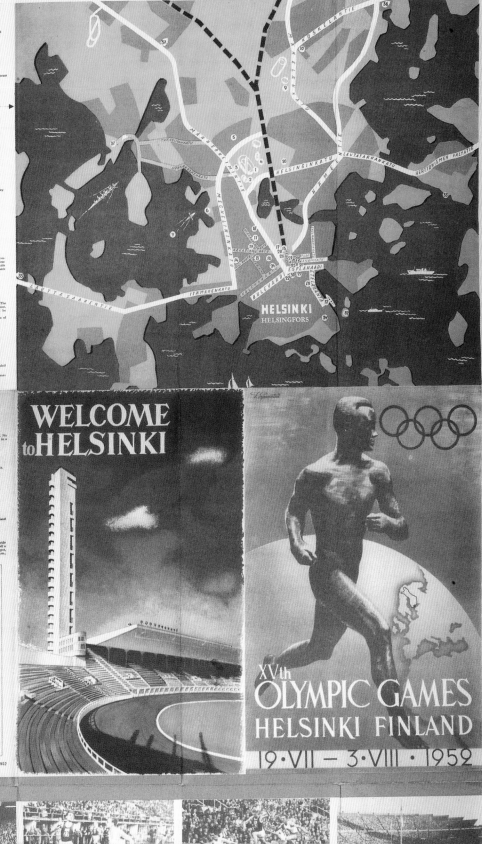

VLADIMIR KUTS (SOVIET UNION)

An athlete who never ran a race until he was 21, this did not stop him from being ranked in the world top ten for 5,000 and 10,000 metres by the age of 24. He out-ran two world record breakers, Emil Zátopek and Christopher Chataway, to win the 1954 European 5,000 metres title in a world record time and subsequently broke that world record three more times.

Kuts also set a world record at 10,000 metres and three at the three mile distance. In his only Olympic appearance in 1956 he won both the 5,000 and 10,000 metres titles. In later years his body suffered from the physically demanding training programme he had undertaken and after a series of heart attacks, he died in 1975 at the age of 48.

Although other athletes had previously won both diving events at the Games, McCormick was the first, female or male, to ever repeat the feat.

On dry land the competitive results were equally impressive as American Robert 'Bobby' Morrow swept the men's 100 and 200 metres athletics events and then added another gold as a member of the American 4 x 100 metres relay team. Not to be outdone, 18-year-old Betty Cuthbert of Australia did the same in the women's events.

Veteran Olympians were also turning out notable performances and adding to their previous results. Frenchman Alain Mimoun managed to gain what had until then been for him an elusive gold by winning the marathon. Hungarian László Papp ended his Olympic career by capturing the gold and in doing so becoming the first boxer to win a total of three gold medals.

Though sport took centre stage, the impact of world events and politics became, not for the first time, intertwined with the celebration. While East and West Germany came together to form the 'United Team of Germany', the Suez crisis and Soviet invasion of Hungary led to a boycott by a few countries. Additionally, tensions spilled over into the pool during the Hungary versus Soviet Union water polo match.

Politics could not, however, stop examples of fair play from occurring. In the 3,000 metres steeplechase the athletes ultimately decided what was fair as Norwegian Ernst Larsen and Hungarian Sándor Rozsnyói objected to the disqualification of Christopher Brasher of Great Britain.

Politics could also not stop the introduction of a new Olympic tradition. At the suggestion of John Ian Wing, the athletes entered the stadium together during the Closing Ceremony as a symbol of global unity.

74

◀ Soviet champion Vladimir Kuts waves as he victoriously crosses the finish line of the Olympic 10,000 metres.

▼ Having had time to change clothes, France's Alain Mimoun is carried in triumph after his marathon victory in Melbourne. The race was run in temperatures which peaked at 97°F (36°C).

▲ Australia's Shirley Strickland on her way to winning the 80 metres hurdles in a new Olympic record time of 10.8 seconds.

◀ Bobby Morrow shares the winners' podium with fellow American Thane Baker and Australian Hector Hogan following his victory in the 100 metres

▼ A Cadbury's chocolate box with a view of Melbourne, the Olympic rings and the city's coat of arms which includes the image of a kangaroo rising above the shield.

JEUX DE LA XVII OLYMPIADE
ROMA ◎◎◎ 25.VIII-11.IX
ROMA MCMLX

ROME 1960

Fifty-four years after Rome gave up on their plans to host the 1908 Games the city received a second chance and did itself proud, organizing a celebration that showed off both its historic roots and modern style.

XVII OLYMPIAD

Opening date: 25 August 1960
Closing date: 11 September 1960
Country of host city: Italy (ITA)
Candidate cities: Lausanne (SUI), Brussels
(BEL), Budapest (HUN), Detroit USA),
Mexico City (MEX), Tokyo (JPN)
Nations: 83
Events: 150

76

◄ Official Olympic poster was created by the Italian artist Armando Testa. The Organizing Committee chose his project from amongst 212 others for the novelty of its graphic expression and its theme. It portrays the apotheosis of a victorious athlete putting on his crown. The well-known Belvedere capital brings Rome's long history of Roman sporting heritage to the fore. The capital is surmounted by the Roman She-wolf which was chosen as the official emblem of the Rome Olympiad.

◣ Torch, designed by Professor Amadeo Maiuri, then Superintendent of Antiquities in Campania. It was inspired by the torches reproduced on ancient monuments. The final bearer was Giancarlo Peris, an Italian track athlete of Greek descent.

In 1960, Rome quite literally welcomed the world as athletes from even more nations participated and, thanks to television, the Games reached a wider global audience. Whether in Rome or as far away as Japan and North America, spectators watched the Games unfold live or with only slight delays on black and white television. By whichever means spectators ended up experiencing the celebration, the Games of the XVII Olympiad provided their global audience with many memorable moments.

The events were made even more striking due to the magical backdrop of the locations that the Organizing Committee chose for the competitions. Venues included a mix of both unforgettable classical settings and modern new sporting facilities. It would have been no surprise if spectators had said they thought they had heard the faint whisper of ancient Roman voices as they witnessed the wrestling events that took place under the remaining vaults of the Basilica of Maxentius. It would also have been no surprise to hear how impressed they had been by the modern, sleek designs of newly built facilities such as the Palazzetto dello Sport.

Inside the newly built Olympic Stadium it all came down to the wire in the last sub-event of the decathlon, the 1,500 metres.

► A plan of the host city showing the different Olympic venues, together with Rome's famous antique sites, temples and ruins.

▲▼ The 1960 Olympic Games was where Cassius Clay first came to the world's attention. He told everybody that he would win gold and did. Shown here are replicas of the boots he wore on his way to the light heavyweight title.

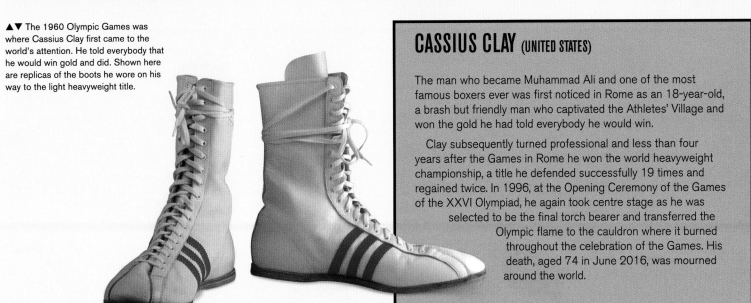

CASSIUS CLAY (UNITED STATES)

The man who became Muhammad Ali and one of the most famous boxers ever was first noticed in Rome as an 18-year-old, a brash but friendly man who captivated the Athletes' Village and won the gold he had told everybody he would win.

Clay subsequently turned professional and less than four years after the Games in Rome he won the world heavyweight championship, a title he defended successfully 19 times and regained twice. In 1996, at the Opening Ceremony of the Games of the XXVI Olympiad, he again took centre stage as he was selected to be the final torch bearer and transferred the Olympic flame to the cauldron where it burned throughout the celebration of the Games. His death, aged 74 in June 2016, was mourned around the world.

Both friends and rivals, Chuan-Kwang Yang of Chinese Taipei and Rafer Johnson of the United States ultimately finished 1-2 in the 1,500. Based on points accumulated in all 10 of the sub-events, however, the gold for the decathlon went to Johnson and the silver to Yang.

The marathon route took athletics out of stadium and on to the streets of Rome for a mini-tour of ancient history. It started at the most sacred of the city's seven hills, the Capitoline, with its Piazza designed by Michelangelo. The route eventually passed along the Appian Way and ended at the Arch of Constantine. For Ethiopian Abebe Bikila, the historical monuments flashed passed as his time of 2:15:16.2 was a world best and he finished the race almost 25 seconds ahead of silver medalist Rhadi ben Abdesselem of Morocco.

Under the modern lines of the Palazzo dello Sport venue American Cassius Clay, who later converted to Islam and changed his name to Muhammad Ali, made his one and only appearance in the Olympic boxing ring. As quick on his feet as he was with his poetry, Clay emulated one of his trademark phrases, to "float like a butterfly and sting like a bee", winning Olympic gold in the light-heavyweight event against Zbigniew Pietrzykowski of Poland.

Gymnastics events were held in the picturesque and historic ruins of the Caracalla Baths. There, in an incredibly tight competition, Takashi Ono of Japan battled it out with Boris

Shakhlin of the Soviet Union in the men's individual all-around event. For Ono, Rome was a case of déjà vu as, just like in Melbourne in 1956, a mere margin of 0.05 points prevented him from gaining the title. Nonetheless, in his third appearance at the Games, Ono continued to add to his Olympic medal collection. Shakhlin did the same and by the end of both of their respective Olympic careers they had collected an impressive total of 13 medals apiece.

Outside of Rome the yachting competitions that were held on the waters of the Bay of Naples also contributed to the list of memorable moments for the 1960 Games. A future king, Crown Prince Constantine of Greece won gold in the dragon event and Paul Elvstrøm of Denmark took home his fourth Olympic gold in his fourth of eight Olympic appearances. History was also made when Peder Lunde Jr., whose father Peder had won silver in 1952 and grandfather Eugene gold in 1924, won his own gold in the Flying Dutchman event. It is, to this day, the only case of a father, son and grandson winning medals in a single sport at the Olympic Games.

The Games in Rome not only made a link between the ancient and modern faces of the city but also a link to the first Games of the modern Olympiad. Following the 1958 decision of the IOC to officially adopt the anthem of Spiros Samaras and Kostis Palamas that had first been played in Athens in 1896, it was once again heard at a celebration of the Games of the Olympiad.

◀ Abebe Bikila became the first African to win gold and won despite running bare-foot in the marathon.

▶ A cloth patch showing a selection of the participating nations' flags, the She-wolf breastfeeding Remus and Romulus, and Rome's principal landmark, the Colosseum.

ABEBE BIKILA (ETHIOPIA)

Abebe Bikila, a member of Emperor Haile Selassie's Imperial Palace Bodyguard, ran the uneven, sometimes cobbled streets of Rome bare-footed simply because the new shoes he had bought to run in did not comfortably fit his feet. It was only his third marathon but nonetheless he ran it in a world best time.

Four years later in Tokyo, roughly just five weeks after having an appendix removed, he again won the gold, this time wearing shoes to improve on the world best time.

During his running career he entered a total of 15 races, completed 13, and won 12 of them. Sadly, Bikila's career was cut short soon after the 1968 Olympic Games when he was involved in a car accident. He was subsequently confined to a wheelchair and died of a brain haemorrhage, at the age of 41.

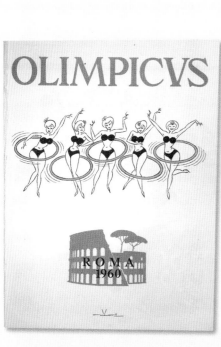

OLIMPICVS

ROMA 1960

▲ For the first time medals were set in a laurel wreath circle and came with a matching chain. This allowed them to be easily worn by the victorious athletes.

◀ An Italian comic released at the time of the Games.

◀ The powerful sprinter Wilma Rudolph became the first American woman to win three golds at a single Olympiad. She triumphed in the 100 metres, 200 metres and 4 x 100 metres relay.

▲ American Rafer Johnson adds to his points total on his way to a decathlon gold medal with a 15.82 metre shot put throw.

TOKYO 1964

The Olympic Games took place in Asia for the first time as the city of Tokyo showed off a new Japan and the Games reflected a wave of technological advances.

◀ One of the four official posters designed by Yusaku Kamekura. It is representative of the national flag of Japan with its rising sun. The official posters received a number of prizes for their excellence, including the Milan Poster Design Award.

XVIII OLYMPIAD
Opening date: 10 October 1964
Closing date: 24 October 1964
Country of host city: Japan (JPN)
Candidate cities: Detroit, (USA) Vienna (AUT), Brussels (BEL)
Nations: 93
Events: 163

In 1964, the Olympic Games were celebrated in Asia for the first time when the Japanese city of Tokyo was selected to act as host. For Tokyo, however, it was a second opportunity, one that they had originally been given for 1940 but later bowed out of due to war. With this second chance, Tokyo welcomed the world to a modern, new Japan and introduced its own people to all that was Olympic.

The whole of Japan and not just Tokyo received this introduction to the Games and its symbols. Such was the enthusiasm of the Japanese public that they bought more than 1.8 million tickets to the events. When the Olympic flame reached Japan it was divided amongst four torches so that it could be carried over four different routes in the country. In this way the flame was shared with as many Japanese citizens as possible before it was once again reunited in a ceremony that took place in the Imperial Palace Plaza the day before the Games were officially opened.

When the Games opened on 10 October 1964 the world received its own introduction to a 'new' Japan that had recovered from war and emerged as a modern country. Looking back, the Games of Tokyo are remembered as much for the futuristic rooftop lines of its national gymnasium buildings as for its link to the technological advances such as coloured television and satellite transmissions that were beamed around the world.

▶ The graphic style of the 1964 Olympic Games was used on a number of items of memorabilia. This fan shows it being utilized on the most traditional of Japanese objects.

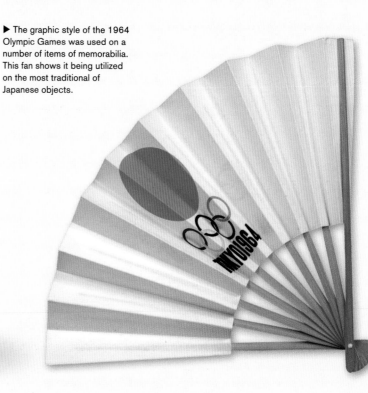

▲▶◥ Tokyo's torch was designed by Sori Yanagi in aluminium to limit its weight. The final torch bearer was Yoshinori Sakai, who was known as the 'Baby from Hiroshima', on account of his being born the day of the atomic explosion. His presence represented peace and hope. All participants in the torch relay wore this white shirt with the Games' emblem.

LARISA LATYNINA (SOVIET UNION)

The record of this athlete positioned her as one of the greatest Olympic gymnasts of all time. Competing in three editions of the Games, she won 18 Olympic medals, nine of them gold. She won an additional eight gold medals at world championships. Her Olympic record was eclipsed by American swimmer Michael Phelps, who finished with 28 medals between 2004 and 2016.

Latynina trained from the age of 11 as a ballet dancer and it was her elegance that drew the eye as much as her technical skill. She was a national schools gymnastics champion at 16 and one of the world's top gymnasts, female or male, in the 1950s and 1960s.

◄◄ Larisa Latynina won two gold medals in the gymnastic disciplines in Tokyo, adding to the seven she won in Melbourne and Rome.

◄ Forty years after it was first designed and cast, Giuseppe Cassioli's medal design was still being used.

▼ Robert 'Bullet Bob' Hayes won the 100 metres and equalled the world record of that day with a time of 10.0 seconds

Multiple medal performances were achieved by athletes such as swimmer Don Schollander and Czech gymnast Vera Caslavska who won four and three golds respectively. For other athletes, it was consecutive wins that made their performances notable. New Zealander Peter Snell defended his 800 metres athletics title, Hungarian water polo player Dezo Gyarmati took home his fifth gold medal and Soviet rower Vyacheslav Ivanov won the men's singles sculls for a third time.

There were also unexpected performances by athletes such as William 'Billy' Mills and Ann Packer. Competing in the 10,000 metres, American Mills improved on his personal best by 46 seconds and won Olympic gold over pre-race favourite Ron Clarke who finished third. Due to the fact that 37 other runners had yet to finish the race, however, Mills' lap of victory had to wait until his return to the stadium 20 years later. In the women's 800 metres it was Packer of Great Britain who won gold in an Olympic record in a distance she had only rarely raced in before Tokyo.

The history made in Japan included more than just new technology, multiple medals and consecutive or unexpected wins. There were also, in fact, several history making sports and participation related firsts or lasts.

The 1964 Olympic programme, for example, was expanded with the first time inclusion of the sports of judo and volleyball.

Judo was a natural choice for inclusion as its origins were rooted in the martial arts of Japan. Four categories were introduced into the competition and it was expected that the Japanese athletes would shine in those events. The fact that volleyball, on the other hand, had been invented in the United States did little to stop it from becoming a highlight of the Games for the Japanese people.

On the judo mats the results were much as expected as Takehide Nakatani, Isao Inokuma and Isao Okano each captured gold. In the open category, however, those with expectations were in for what should not have been such as a surprise as a two-time world champion Antonius 'Anton' Geesink of the Netherlands took gold over Japan's Akio Kaminaga.

Even before gold was won on the court, team captain Masae Kasai and the rest of the Japanese women's volleyball team were already household names. It was no surprise then that the country almost ground to a halt as its people gathered around television sets or attended the final match and saw these dedicated women win gold over a team from the Soviet Union.

Statistics for the 1964 Olympic Games also demonstrated that global changes caused by a number of colonies becoming independent in the years leading up to Tokyo had an impact on the number of participating nations. As a result, the number increased by 10 and athletes from countries such as Senegal, Niger and Mali made their first Olympic appearance. At the same time, South Africa's invitation to participate at the Games was withdrawn due to the country's apartheid policy. The same reason resulted in Southern Rhodesia, competing under the name Rhodesia, participating for its last time until 1980 when the newly-independent nation made its debut under the name Zimbabwe.

▼▶ Judo was an Olympic sport for the first time during these Games and Dutchman Anton Geesink won the gold medal defeating Akio Kaminaga with a *kesa-gatame* hold. Shown here is a commemorative glass celebrating his Olympic triumph.

東京都区内私鉄優待乗車証
FREE PASS FOR PRIVATE RAILWAY LINES
IN TOKYO AREA

1. 持参人　1名
   Good for 'Holder only.

2. 有効区間　裏面表示の赤線区間
   Lines available : Lines indicated in red ink.
   (See the reverse side map)

3. 有効期間　昭和39年9月25日〜11月5日
   Period : September 25 – November 5 1964

東京私鉄協讃連合会
Liaison Council of Private Railways in Tokyo

TOKYO 1964

№ 005684

RADIO & T·V
TOKYO 1964
10
NO RT 6721 4
SEAT 19
TIME

OPENING CEREMONY
NATIONAL STADIUM

▲ Radio-TV accreditation card for the Opening Ceremony in the National stadium.

◀ Free pass for railway lines in the Tokyo area.

第18回
オリンピック
競技大会

THE GAMES
OF THE XVIII
OLYMPIAD
TOKYO
1964

開会式
OPENING CEREMONY

国立競技場　NATIONAL STADIUM

1010
10月 OCTOBER
10日

特等　CLASS-S

席　SEAT

2　前段
LOW

T-14

▲ An entry ticket for the Games in Tokyo. Just over two million tickets were sold in total. The graphic style created by Yusaku Kamekura was followed throughout all the official documents.

◤ Swimmer Don Schollander became the first American to win four golds at a single Games since Jesse Owens in Berlin 1936.

▷ Overleaf: Peter Snell crosses the finish line in advance of the pack to win gold in Tokyo.

DONALD 'DON' SCHOLLANDER (UNITED STATES)

Born in Oregon but trained as a swimmer in Santa Clara, California, Don Schollander became the first swimmer to capture four gold medals at a single edition of the Games. The victories came in Tokyo in the 100 and 400 metres freestyle as well as in the 4 x 100 and 4 x 200 metres freestyle relays.

Four years later, in Mexico, he swam in the 200 metres freestyle, an event in which he broke the world record eight times in five years, setting a world record in the trials. He took home silver in the event and then rounded out his Olympic career by winning gold as a member of the US men's 4 x 200 metres relay team.

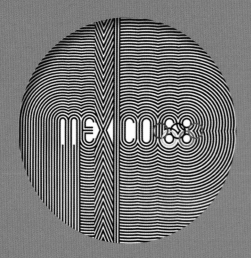

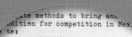

methods to bring anu...
...dition for competition in Mex.
...te to:
    a. acclimatisation-period in Mex.
    tition
    b. training - schedules
    c. way of living in Mexico (living ha...

To define precautions to be taken if necessary,
food and drink to avoid gastrointestinal infecti...

Methods:

Testees: 5 female athletes
        5 male athletes
        2 female non-athletes
        2 male non-athletes

Athletes were chosen from the following sports e...
                athle...
                swim...
                can...
                cy...

...n non-athletes were made to disti...
...f training and of acclimatis...

Bayer. Staatsministerium des Innern

(40/72) 7.September 1972

Erste Zusammenfassung über den wesentlichen Ablauf der
Ereignisse im Zusammenhang mit der Geiselnahme israelisc...
Sportler durch arabische Terroristen am 5.September und i...
der Nacht vom 5. zum 6.September 1972.

Um 5.00 Uhr und 3 Minuten kam die erste telefonische Meldu...
aus dem Olympischen Dorf bei der Polizei an: "Es wird gesc...
sen." Im Bau 31 sollten drei Araber auf Israelis in deren
Unterkunft das Feuer eröffnet haben. Einem fünf Minuten sp...
eintreffenden leitenden Polizeibeamten des Polizeiführungs...
stabes übergaben die Täter ein Ultimatum mit der Forderun...
200 arabische Häftlinge freizulassen. Es wurde eine Fris...
9.00 Uhr gestellt. Die Polizei traf sofort umfangreiche...
sperrungsmaßnahmen und verständigte alle infragekommen...
...dienststellen. Vor dem Bau 31 wurde eine Mitarbeiter...
...gradienstes, die Kriminalbeamtin ist, postiert.
...Funkgerät ausgerüstet. Sie hatte den Auft...
...Einsatzleitung zu halten. Gleichzei...
...zum Olympischen Dorf beord...
...allgemeinen

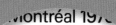

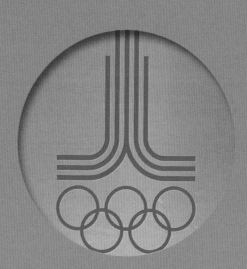

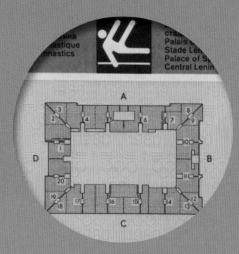

CHAPTER 4

THE GAMES IN CHANGING TIMES

Even as the world outside of sport left its mark on the celebration of Olympic Games, the Games themselves continued. Politics, social protest, tragedy and boycotts became a part of Games' history, but so too did the introduction of visual identities for a Games edition, celebrations of culture, modernistic architecture for venues and revolutionary innovations. Competition remained at the heart of the Games though, as athletes achieved unimaginable results, setting new records along the way.

MEXICO 1968

The Games of the XIX Olympiad provided spectators with a combination of high octane, low oxygen record breaking surprises, talented performances, and cultural delights as Mexico welcomed the world.

XIX OLYMPIAD

Opening date: 12 October 1968

Closing date: 27 October 1968

Country of host city: Mexico (MEX)

    Candidate cities: Buenos Aires (ARG),

    Detroit (USA), Lyon (FRA)

Nations: 112

Events: 172

◄ Based on Pedro Ramirez Vazquez's original idea to combine the year 68 with the Olympic rings, the artists Eduardo Terrazas and Lance Wyman created a distinctive style. It recalls the concentric motifs of the Huichole Indians, the work of Victor Vasarely and the kinetic art in general. Here it is shown developed as the official poster.

◤ There were three types of torch produced in Mexico. The one shown here was used by the last relay runner.

▼ For the first time at the Games of the Olympiad, the last torch bearer was a woman, the Mexican athlete Enriqueta Basilio de Sotelo.

A look back at the history of the 1968 Olympic Games that took place in Mexico City is most often linked to photographic images of Bob Beamon leaping through the air or the 'Black Power' salute of American sprinters Tommie Smith and John Carlos. The highlights of these Games, however, included more than just the impacts of politics and the effects of altitude on athletic performances.

One of the most striking sights of the Games was the way in which the organizers contributed their own unique visual identity to the Games, one that incorporated both modern graphics and Mexican cultural heritage. While previous Olympic hosts had also introduced their culture into the Games' atmosphere, what made Mexico historically significant was that their 'look' was reflected throughout the Games. The Mexico logotype became the foundation for the design on items such as the posters, torches, uniforms and even in the painted design of the Olympic Stadium plaza.

Culture as well as history played an influential role in defining the overall programme of the Games. For the first time in Olympic history, an Organizing Committee decided to host an arts festival that lasted for one year rather than just for the

▼ An Opening Ceremony admission ticket. The graphics used for the Olympic alphabet reflect the same style as that used for the Games' emblem.

JAMES 'JIM' HINES (UNITED STATES)

One man who refused to accept that altitude helped was Jim Hines who won the 100 metres in a world record of 9.95 seconds. Tests showed that there was 23 percent less air density but Hines said: "It was the only time in my life that I finished a race and felt absolutely dead." Hines won a second gold as a member of the US men's 4 x 100 metres relay team, also in world record time.

Mexico was his first and last Olympic appearance as he went on from there to become a professional football player, signing up with the Miami Dolphins. His name would remain in the record books for a long time though as his 100 metres record-breaking time stood for almost 15 years.

duration of the Games. The 500-plus events of the festival were rich in both Mexican and international content and highlighted examples of the arts such as dance, poetry and folk art as well as science and architecture.

The cultural programme placed an equally high emphasis on the young. As such, there was also an international youth camp, a festival of children's painting, a film festival and a reception by Mexico's youth to the youth of the world.

For the sporting community the choice of Mexico was not, however, welcomed by all due to concerns over the challenge that the city's high-altitude location would present to the athletes.

The examples that are most often recalled when discussion today turns to talk of the benefits of altitude on the sporting competitions from 1968 are those of the athletics sprint and jumping events. In the men's triple jump, for example, an eight-year-old world record was broken five times, with the last being by Soviet athlete Viktor Saneev who won with a 17.39-metre jump that was an improvement of 36 centimetres over the pre-Games mark. In the men's 400 metres, American Lee Evans set a record of 43.85 seconds that was to last 20 years.

The results of Mexico should not merely be attributed to the impact of altitude, however, as weather made for a challenging equestrian competition and new techniques and equipment as well as the natural talent of the athletes also led to notable performances.

▼ Jim Hines celebrates his win in the 100 metres with his team mate Charles Greene.

▼ All-round gymnastics champion Vera Caslavska on the uneven bars, one of three individual apparatus on which she won gold medals.

▲ A golden Adidas sprint shoe worn by the 100 metres champion Jim Hines when he anchored the US 4 x 100 metres relay team to a world record.

BOB BEAMON (UNITED STATES)

Never has a performance proved so shocking as that of Bob Beamon's long jump of 8.90 metres, and not least of all to the New Yorker himself. When it was explained to him that the metric mark on the scoreboard converted to 29ft 2½ inches, his legs collapsed under him.

Judges were just as surprised. The optical measuring device slid off its rail before it reached the point of his impact, and they had to call for a steel measuring tape.

"Compared to his jump, we are all children," said Soviet rival Igor Ter-Ovanesyan. Beamon's jump improved on the world record by 55 centimetres and was to last for almost 23 years.

In the equestrian three day event conditions went from being merely a competition to a matter of survival as constant rain turned the cross country course into a treacherous challenge for both horse and rider alike. France's Jean-Jacques Guyon and his horse Pitou became only the second French entry to win gold in the event but sadly two horses were lost to the difficult conditions.

The revolution in the high jump was purely athletic as American Richard 'Dick' Fosbury used a new technique, later dubbed the 'Fosbury Flop', in which he pivoted on take-off to clear the bar head first. It won him Olympic gold, but only by two centimetres.

On the running track, competitors benefited from the first Olympic use of an artificial running surface. Rain proved no obstacle with the new surface and for athletes the springy surface also translated into fewer injuries such as shin splints. In the pool, swimmers benefited from more accurate results as timing advances led to the first use of electronic touch plates at

▲ So long was Bob Beamon's first jump that the optical measuring device slid off its rail before it reached the point of impact.

▶ The design of this hostesses' uniform is taken from the Games' emblem. The colour scheme chosen for the items created for the Games was lively, joyful and playful.

▼ Longines digital display chronometer. Mexico was the first Olympic Summer Games with fully automatic time-keeping.

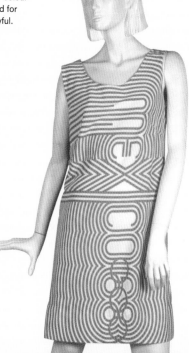

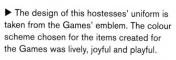

▲ The effects of altitude proved challenging for some athletes competing in the endurance type sports in Mexico.

▶ Tommie Smith and John Carlos waited for the first note of the American anthem to lift their gloved fists in protest at US Black oppression.

LONGINES OLYMPIC TIMING

◀ This would be the last time that Giuseppe Cassioli's medal design of 1928 would appear unmodified. A renovated design of the reverse was to be commissioned for the 1972 Olympic Games.

▶ Extract from a medical report on strenuous exercise at high altitude in response to concerns that it would endanger athletes' health.

▼ Few can be truly credited for revolutionizing an Olympic event but Dick Fosbury's pioneering 'flop' won him the gold and transformed the high jump forever.

▷ Overleaf: In his first Olympic appearance Marc Spitz (centre) took home silver in the men's 100m butterfly event.

Summary of the investigations carried out by Prof. dr. P.A. Biersteker to the order of the Netherlands Olympic Committee.

Commission:

To carry out investigations to determine the effects of altitude on maximum performance in Mexico City.

To determine possible harmful effects and the measures which should be taken to avoid these.

To investigate methods to bring and keep participants in optimal condition for competition in Mexico with special reference to:
     a. acclimatisation-period in Mexico prior to competition
     b. training - schedules
     c. way of living in Mexico (living habits)

To define precautions to be taken if necessary, concerning food and drink to avoid gastrointestinal infections.

Methods:

Testees: 5 female athletes
        5 male athletes
        2 female non-athletes
        2 male non-athletes

Athletes were chosen from the following sports events:
          athletics
          swimming
          canoeing
          cycling

Tests on non-athletes were made to distinguish between the effects of training and of acclimatisation in Mexico City.

Investigations carried out in Holland during a period of 4 weeks (15 aug. - 15 sept. 1966).

1. Each testee was tested once a week on the bicycle-ergometer by means of an increased work-load test. On fixed points during performance and recovery period (see appended scheme) registrations were made concerning:
          E.C.G.
          pulse-rate
          blood pressure
          breathing frequency
          minute volume

Venous blood samples (dorsal hand vein) were taken for the determination of:
     Hb - Ht
     Lactic acid
     pH, $pCO_2 + pO_2$, HCO_3^-, Na^o, K^o, Ca^{oo},
     O_2 - saturation.

Gassamples were taken to determine O_2 - consumption and CO_2 - production.

the finish wall that were linked directly with the starter's pistol, leaving less room for the potential of human error.

Talent was assuredly also in evidence in Mexico in events such as gymnastics where Mikhail Voronin won two golds, four silvers and one bronze medal and his wife Zinaida won a gold, a silver and two bronze. Their exploits though were over-shadowed in local headlines by a Czech gymnast, Vera Caslavska. The winner of four gold and two silver medals, Caslavska's Olympic experience in Mexico was made all the more memorable when she chose the city's Metropolitan Cathedral as the place to marry her countryman Josef Odlozil, the 1964 Olympic 1,500 metres silver medalist.

Talent also came in the form of family in the case of Sweden's silver medal winning cycling team time trial entry as the four riders were also brothers; Erik, Sture, Gösta and Tomas Pettersson.

MUNICH 1972

The Games proved their resilience when tragedy in the Olympic Village became mixed with the results of the sporting competitions and the decision was made that "the Games must go on."

◀ The official poster by Otl Aicher communicates the specific spirit of the Games with the design evoking the modern architecture of the Games's sporting venues.

▼ Munich's Olympic torch was manufactured by the firm Krupp which had also created the torch for the 1936 Berlin Olympic Games. The torch had a burning duration of 20 minutes. German athlete Günter Zahn had the honour of being the last runner in the torch relay.

XX OLYMPIAD

Opening date: 26 August 1972
Closing date: 11 September 1972
Country of host city: Federal Republc of
    Germany (FRG)
Candidate cities: Detroit (USA), Madrid (ESP),
    Montreal (CAN)
Nations: 121
Events: 195

On 26 August 1972 the people of Munich welcomed the world to the Opening Ceremony of what organizers had planned to be a joyful, friendly and colourful celebration of the Games of the XX Olympiad. It would have been hard to imagine then that 11 days later the festive atmosphere and the history making performances of the athletes, although still a defining part of the Games, would be diminished.

That is exactly what happened, however, when eight terrorists, representing the militant group 'Black September', managed to enter the Olympic Village in the early morning hours of 5 September. The terrorists killed two members of the Israeli delegation and took nine more hostage. In a failed rescue attempt, the nine Israeli hostages were killed along with one German policeman and five of the terrorists. The Games were

▲ The Adidas trainers worn by Kipchoge 'Kip' Keino when he broke the 3,000 metres steeplechase Olympic record in Munich. The sole was partially cut and some shark skin was applied. This was supposed to provide an improved grip when the foot was underwater.

MARK SPITZ (UNITED STATES)

With a body that his coach described as "purpose built for swimming" Mark Spitz recovered from his personal disappointment of 1968 in Mexico City to do in 1972 in Munich what no athlete in any sport had ever done before at the Olympic Games. There, he became the first competitor in Olympic history to win six gold medals at the same Games when he won the 100 metres freestyle. He then went one better by winning a seventh as a member of the US men's 4 x 100 metres medley relay team.

Over his entire swimming career Spitz set 26 individual world records, competed in two Olympic Games and won a total of 10 Olympic medals, nine of them gold. He was also a member of six world record setting relay teams.

suspended and a memorial service was held in the Olympic Stadium but it was ultimately decided by the International Olympic Committee that in defiance of this act of terrorism, "the Games must go on."

Thus, the history of the Munich Games became a bittersweet mix of tragedy and triumph in the face of adversity. The notable performances of some of the athletes would come to be remembered even today for not only being set against the backdrop of the architectural modernity of the Olympic venues but also against the sorrow and sense of loss.

In a pool that was made for records, thanks to its revolutionary gutter system and ripple reducing lane markers, Mark Spitz still managed to make waves when he won seven golds, all in world record time. In the women's events Shane Gould of Australia put on her own show as she won gold in the 200 metres individual medley as well as the 200 and 400 metres freestyle events, a silver in the 800 metres freestyle and a bronze in the 100 metres freestyle, setting three world and one Olympic record along the way. A year later, at the young age of 16, Gould retired from competition.

Youth also had its place in the athletics competitions, although so too did experience. In the women's high jump 16-year-old Ulrike Meyfarth of the Federal Republic of Germany jumped higher than she ever had before, clearing 1.92m to set both an Olympic record and equal the world record.

▼ 'Waldi', the dachshund, became the first official mascot. His colour scheme was inatended to express the joy of the Olympic festival.

▶ Aged just 16, West German athlete Ulrike Meyfarth became the youngest ever women's Olympic high jump champion. Twelve years later she would triumph again in Los Angeles.

▶ The winner's medal designed by a former teacher at the Weimar Bauhaus, Gerhard Marcks. The reverse, shown here, uses a representative image of Castor and Pollux, the twin sons of Zeus and Léda, the patrons of sports competitions and friendship. The Organizing Committee for the Games in Munich in 1972 broke new ground by having a different reverse. The obverse shows Cassioli's design, first used in 1928.

Her performance also earned her a distinction that is still hers even to this day, that of being the youngest ever competitor, male of female, to have won individual Olympic athletics gold. Meanwhile, making a fourth appearance at the Olympic Games, 40-year-old Mamo Wolde of Ethiopia completed his medal collection, gaining a bronze in the marathon to add to his 1968 marathon Olympic gold medal as well as the silver he won in the 10,000 metres in Mexico City.

In the gymnastics venue, it was Soviet newcomer Olga Korbut who captured the hearts of the media and the fans with both the ups and downs of her performance and set the stage for other gymnastics 'munchkins' to come in later editions of the Games.

Other noteworthy performances in the gymnastics were made by those for whom the Games in Munich were not their first Olympic appearances. Karin Janz of the German Democratic Republic added two silvers in the team and individual all-around competitions as well as two golds and one bronze in the apparatus events to the bronze and silver she had already won in Mexico. In the men's competition, Sawao Kato of Japan added three gold and two silver medals to the individual all-around and team golds as well as the one gold and one bronze in the apparatus events he too had already won in Mexico.

The Olympic programme saw both the return of archery with an individual event for men as well as for women and men's handball. In archery, the results were again a mix of young and old as 18-year-old reigning world champion John Williams won the men's competition and 42-year-old Doreen Wilber won the women's.

Four slalom kayak and Canadian events were also introduced for the first time to the programme. Fittingly, it was a contingent of athletes from both East and West Germany that made Olympic history in Munich as they paddled their way to top finishes on a man-made course that featured artificial rapids.

▲▶ A mix of memorabilia commissioned for the 1972 Olympic Games. Shown here are cigar labels featuring some of the stars of the Games and a branded bottle-opener.

◀ Flowers placed in memorial outside Connollystrasse 31 where Israeli athletes, coaches and officials had been taken hostage.

▶ Part of a detailed initial summary of the sequence of events in connection with the taking of Israeli athletes as hostages by Arab terrorists on 5 September 1972.

presse rundfunk und fernsehen für presse rundfunk und fernsehen für presse rundfunk und fernsehen für presse rundfunk und fernsehen

Bayer. Staatsministerium des Innern

(140/72)   7.September 1972

Erste Zusammenfassung über den wesentlichen Ablauf der Ereignisse im Zusammenhang mit der Geiselnahme israelischer Sportler durch arabische Terroristen am 5.September und in der Nacht vom 5. zum 6.September 1972.

Um 5.00 Uhr und 3 Minuten kam die erste telefonische Meldung aus dem Olympischen Dorf bei der Polizei an: "Es wird geschossen." Im Bau 31 sollten drei Araber auf Israelis in deren Unterkunft das Feuer eröffnet haben. Einem fünf Minuten später eintreffenden leitenden Polizeibeamten des Polizeiführungsstabes übergaben die Täter ein Ultimatum mit der Forderung, 200 arabische Häftlinge freizulassen. Es wurde eine Frist bis 9.00 Uhr gestellt. Die Polizei traf sofort umfangreiche Absperrungsmaßnahmen und verständigte alle infragekommenden Dienststellen. Vor dem Bau 31 wurde eine Mitarbeiterin des Ordnungsdienstes, die Kriminalbeamtin ist, postiert. Sie wurde mit einem Funkgerät ausgerüstet. Sie hatte den Auftrag, die Verbindung zur Einsatzleitung zu halten. Gleichzeitig wurden Präzisionsschützen zum Olympischen Dorf beordert. Die Lerchenauerstraße wurde für den allgemeinen Fahrverkehr gesperrt. Eine Einsatzleitung wurde im Olympischen Dorf aufgebaut.

Um 7.20 Uhr traf der bayerische Innenminister Dr.Bruno Merk und kurz darauf der Bundesinnenminister Hans Dietrich Genscher im Olympischen Dorf ein.

Nach 8.00 Uhr erging die Weisung an den Polizeiführungsstab, die Befreiung der Geiseln einsatztaktisch vorzubereiten.

In Verhandlungen mit den Terroristen erreichte der Polizeipräsident, daß das zunächst bis 9.00 Uhr befristete Ultimatum

8 münchen 22 odeonsplatz 3 telefon (0811) 2192/208 od. 725 ministerialrat heinrich v.mosch telex bymdi mchn (05) 524 540

OLGA KORBUT (SOVIET UNION)

Tiny Olga Korbut, nicknamed the 'Munchkin of Munich' by the US press, captivated audiences without dominating her rivals. She won two individual apparatus gold as well as a gold in the team competition. Despite a seventh-place finish in the individual all-around competition, her spectacular routines made her famous in an instant.

She had to adopt a disguise to visit shops in Munich and once back in the Soviet Union the local post office had to assign a clerk just to handle her fan mail. She was team leader of the Soviet team in Montreal four years later, won a team gold and one more silver. She settled in America after the break-up of the Soviet Union.

▸ Olga Korbut's spectacular routines caught the mood of the Munich crowd making her one of the stars of the Games.

▼ In controversial circumstances, the USA suffered their first basketball defeat in Olympic history against the team from the USSR in the 1972 final.

▸ Finn Lasse Viren won two golds in Munich, in the 5,000 and 10,000 metres events.

MONTREAL 1976

A perfect '10' turned a gymnastics 'pixie' into an international star and even a rugby union tour could not stop the avalanche of impressive history-in-the-making moments in the athletics events.

◀ The official poster is entitled 'The Invitation' and represents the five rings reflected symbolically by successive waves. It invited the athletes of the world to the 1976 Olympic Games.

XXI OLYMPIAD

Opening date: 17 July 1976
Closing date: 1 August 1976
Country of host city: Canada (CAN)
Candidate cities: Moscow (URS), Los Angeles (USA)
Nations: 92
Events: 198

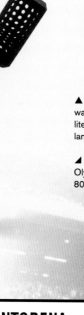

◣ Created by Georges Huel and Michel Dallaire, the Montreal Olympic torch was constructed from aluminium to limit its weight and used olive oil for the fuel. The final torch bearers were two youths who were chosen to symbolise Canada's two founding peoples, an English speaker, Sandra Henderson and a French speaker, Stéphane Préfontaine.

▲ The mascot for the 1976 Games was a beaver named Amik, which literally means 'beaver' in the Algonquin language.

◢ Alberto Juantorena is the only Olympian to win gold in both the 400 and 800 metres events.

The Games of the XXI Olympiad quickly found their rhythm, in spite of an incomplete Olympic Stadium and a boycott by a small number of largely African nations over New Zealand's participation in a rugby union tour of South Africa. Following a festive Opening Ceremony, the spotlight just as quickly shifted from there to a gymnastic 'pixie' from Romania and the history made in such events as athletics and diving.

The sporting history of the Montreal Games came to be most synonymous with the name Nadia and the number '10'. At just 14 years of age and a petite 1.5 metres in height, Nadia Comaneci became the first athlete to score the maximum 10 in Olympic gymnastics competition on the uneven bars. So unexpected was her result that it was not actually possible to show the 10.00 on the scoreboard and instead it was displayed as a 1.00! Before the gymnastics competition had ended Nadia had scored another six perfect 10.0s, won the women's individual all-around title as well as captured golds on the balance beam and the uneven bars, a silver in the team competition and a bronze in the floor exercise event.

ALBERTO JUANTORENA (CUBA)

The only man in Olympic history to win gold medals in both 400 and 800 metres, he was recognizable by his 1.90m tall physique and giant stride. Yet he had to be deceived by his coach into ever running the longer distance, persuaded only by the promise that it would be training for the 400 metres.

Juantorena completed the same double at the following year's World Cup but problems with his Achilles tendon prevented him defending his Olympic titles in 1980. He retired to become Cuba's representative on the IAAF's executive council.

Nadia, however, was not the only star of the Games or the women's gymnastics competitions. Soviet competitor Nelli Kim scored two 10.0s on her way to three gold medals and one silver. Her team mates Olga Korbut and Lyudmila Turischeva also added to the charged atmosphere, proving they could still compete with the youngsters by taking home two and four medals respectively.

In the athletics events, the anticipated impact of the boycott on the middle and distance races proved to be negligible. Instead, performance after performance resulted in the writing of new Olympic history, and not just in the middle and long distance events and not just the men's events either.

Lasse Viren, who had won both the 5,000 and 10,000 metres in Munich, did so again. With this feat he became only the second man after Emil Zátopek to retain the 10,000 metres Olympic title, and the first to repeat as Olympic 5,000 metres champion.

◀ Virtually unknown when he entered the 1976 Olympic marathon, Waldemar Cierpinski went on to win the event by a narrow margin of just under 51 seconds.

▲ The flags of all nations decorate the background at the medal ceremony where American John Naber received gold. He won four golds and one silver at the Games.

▼ Pennant carrying the Games' official emblem. Standing out for its simplicity and the strength, the emblem symbolically combines the letter 'M' for Montreal, a winners' podium, an athletics track and the Olympic rings.

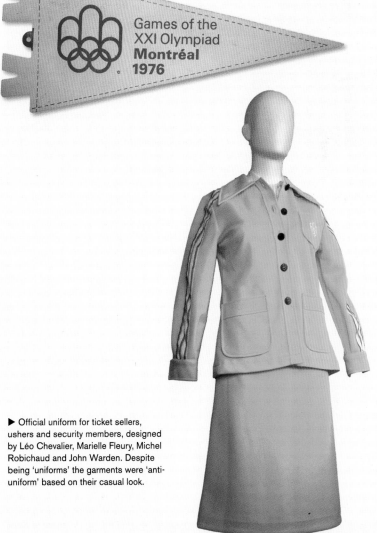

▶ Official uniform for ticket sellers, ushers and security members, designed by Léo Chevalier, Marielle Fleury, Michel Robichaud and John Warden. Despite being 'uniforms' the garments were 'anti-uniform' based on their casual look.

In the shorter distances, impressive performances were turned in by Alberto Juantorena of Cuba and Irena Szewinska of Poland. For Szewinska, an Olympic and world record finish in the women's 400 metres brought her Olympic medal tally to seven in five different events. In the men's 400 metres it was Juantorena who was favoured to win. Before the 400 metres, however, he chose to first compete in the 800 metres where he broke the world record in a time of 1:43.50 and won gold. Four days later he won his specialist event, the 400 metres.

The victory of another Olympic veteran, Hungarian javelin thrower Miklós Németh, was made all the more personally memorable by the fact that he was able to emulate his father, Imre's golden performance in the hammer throw in 1948.

The theme of impressive performances by Olympic veterans continued in the diving pool where Italian Klaus Dibiasi put on a strong show in the men's platform event to finish ahead of a young Greg Louganis of the United States. For Dibiasi, his win earned him a place in the history books as the first diver to have won three consecutive gold medals in a diving event as well as the first to have won four diving medals.

Perhaps not as well known, but equally as noteworthy, was the way in which the Montreal organizers decided to bring the Olympic flame from Greece to Canada. While the Olympic torch has since been taken into space, 1976 was the first and only time that the Olympic flame travelled by air, but not by plane or rocket. Instead, the Flame was carried by relay from Olympia to Athens where it was then turned into coded impulses and then transmitted via satellite to the Canadian capital of Ottawa where it was returned to its original shape through the use of a laser beam.

▲ Hungarian Miklós Németh reacts following his new world record javelin throw of 94.58 metres.

◀ Edwin Moses (right) enjoys a lap of honour after winning the final of the 400 metres hurdles. Pictured with him is American athlete Michael Shine, who won the silver.

▲ The work hat given to IOC representatives on their visit to the Stadium in 1975.

▶ A joy to behold on the beam, Nadia Comaneci would go on to be awarded a perfect 10.0 on the asymmetric bars.

◀ First place winner's medal with its wooden presentation case. The reverse of the medal was deliberately designed to be plain. It included only a stylized laurel crown, a symbol of Victory, and the emblem of the Games.

Programme du parcours de la flamme olympique   Olympic Flame Relay Program

Guide du porteur   **Flame Bearer's Guide**

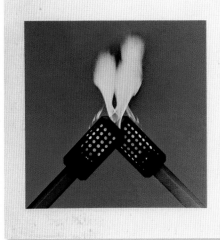

▶ Flame bearer's guide containing instructions on how to carry the torch or transfer the flame.

NADIA COMANECI (ROMANIA)

The first gymnast in Olympic history to score the maximum of 10 on the uneven bars, she was awarded a total of seven during these Games. She came to Montreal with high expectations, having become the youngest at 13 ever to win gold at the European championships the previous year, but seven 10s were beyond prediction.

Her agility took gymnastics to new horizons, and such was her supremacy that she retained her European overall title twice more. She was second in the women's individual all-around event at the 1980 Games and also won two golds on individual apparatus and a silver in the team competition to bring her career total to nine Olympic medals, five of them gold. She defected to the United States in 1989 and later became a respected coach.

MOSCOW 1980

The number of participating nations was reduced to 80 by a US-led boycott but the athletes in attendance still produced many memorable sporting moments.

◄ The official poster for 1980 Moscow, featuring the Games emblem was selected from amongst 26,000 proposals.

◣ Led by Boris Petrovich Tuchin, a dedicated group from Leningrad's Scientific and Industrial unit designed the torch in just two months. Soviet basketball player Sergei Belov had the honour of lighting the Olympic cauldron at the Opening Ceremony.

▼ Ever changing mosaic scenes like the one shown here also featured at the Opening Ceremony for the Olympic Games in Moscow.

XXII OLYMPIAD

Opening date: 19 July 1980
Closing date: 3 August 1980
Country of host city: Soviet Union (URS)
Candidate cities: Los Angeles (USA)
Nations: 80
Events: 203

The selection of Moscow as the host city for the Games of the XXII Olympiad took the celebration to a Communist country for the first time. In between the time of the selection and the Opening Ceremony of the Games the world's athletes and the host city both made preparations. For many of the athletes, however, their preparations did not lead to participation in the Games as the Soviet's invasion of Afghanistan led the then US president Jimmy Carter to call on the world to boycott in protest.

With a large number of nations absent, either due to the boycott or for other reasons such as having no athletes who met qualification standards, it was to be expected that the competition level in some events would be affected. Nonetheless, those who came to participate at the Games proved that they came ready to compete. More world records were broken in Moscow than four years earlier in Montreal and in some cases those who achieved them had been expected to lead their competitions.

▲ 'Misha the Bear' was chosen as the Olympic mascot by 40,000 viewers of a television programme. The final design was designed by Victor Tchijikov.

One such case was that of the much anticipated duel between fellow British middle distance runners Steve Ovett and Sebastian Coe, two men who had re-written the record books in the 15 months preceding the Games. Ovett was favoured for the 1,500 metres, a distance in which he was unbeaten in the three years prior to Moscow. On the other hand, Coe, the world record holder, was expected to win the 800 metres race.

Fate though turned expectations on their head. Whereas Ovett ran a smart race in the 800 metres, Coe ran a bad tactical race. As a result Ovett came away with the gold and Coe with the silver. Ironically, fate was again waiting when the men's 1,500 metres final took place six days later. This time it was Coe who won gold while Ovett took the bronze as they both battled in the homestretch to overtake East Germany's Jürgen Straub who managed to hold on for the silver.

Another Brit, decathlete Francis 'Daley' Thompson, was also an athlete from whom great results were anticipated as he had set a new world record score just three months prior to the Games. Thompson did not disappoint and competing in his second Olympic Games he won his first Olympic gold. Four years later in Los Angeles he repeated the result.

In his third appearance at the Olympic Games, Cuban boxer Teófilo Stevenson established himself as a sporting legend. Competing in the heavyweight category Stevenson put on another memorable performance to capture his third Olympic gold. In doing so he became only the second boxer in Olympic history to have won three golds and the first to have won them consecutively in the same weight category.

◥ Already the world record holder, Italian Pietro Mennea overcame Moscow's 100 metres champion Allan Wells to take the 200 metres title.

▶ Steve Ovett salutes the Moscow crowd following his win over British rival Sebastian Coe in the 800 metres final.

◢ Entry ticket to the gymnastics competitions at the Palace of Sports on 25 July, when Soviet gymnast Aleksandr Dityatin won six medals in a single day.

STEVE OVETT (GREAT BRITAIN)

Steve Ovett was the elder by a year of a pair of middle distance runners from Britain who dominated middle distance running in the period around the early 1980s and traded world records back and forth between them.

Ovett, from Brighton on the English south coast, emerged first in 1975 when he won the European Cup. He remained unbeaten at the 1,500 metres for three years before the Moscow Games when Sebastian Coe beat him.

He set world records at 1,500 metres and twice at one mile, won European and Commonwealth Games titles as well as two Olympic medals, but his career declined after he seriously damaged his leg running into a railing near his home in 1982 and his last Olympic appearance would be a heartbreaking one in Los Angeles in 1984.

The biggest star of the gymnastics competitions was men's individual all-around champion Aleksandr Dityatin of the Soviet Union. In addition to the all-around gold, he won two more in the team and the apparatus rings events. He also won a total of four silver medals in the horizontal bar, parallel bars, pommel horse and vault competitions and a bronze in the floor exercises.

In the canoeing competitions Birgit Fischer, then representing the German Democratic Republic, made her first Olympic appearance and won her first Olympic gold in the women's K-1,500 metres kayak flatwater singles event. With the exception of Los Angeles in 1984, Fischer would go on to compete in every future edition of the Summer Games, up to Athens in 2004, and turn that single Moscow gold into an impressive collection of eight gold and four silver medals.

The Games in Moscow also became known in some events as the Games of identical twins as three sets of them won medals. On the wrestling mats it was Soviet brothers Sergei and Anatoli Beloglazov who, with equally strong results throughout the rounds of the competitions came away with gold. For Sergei, victory came in the bantamweight category and for Anatoli, in the flyweight event.

For rowing spectators who thought that they were seeing double twice in the men's coxless pairs event, they were! Not only did identical twins Bernd and Jörg Landvoigt of the German Democratic Republic repeat their performance of 1976 and take home the gold again, but the silver was also won by identical twins, Yuri and Nikolai Pimenov of the Soviet Union.

MIRUTS YIFTER (ETHIOPIA)

For Ethiopian Air Force officer Miruts Yifter, dubbed 'Yifter the Shifter' because of his fast finishes, the Olympic Games had their high points and their low points.

In 1972 he won a bronze at 10,000 metres but then failed to show for the 5,000 metres final despite having qualified for it. Four years later, his country was among those which boycotted the Montreal Games.

Finally in 1980, after he had won the 5,000 and 10,000 metres at the previous year's World Cup, everything went right for him. Already a father of six and believed to be at least 35 years of age, he ran the final 200 metres of the men's 5,000 metres race in a remarkable 27.2 seconds and the last 200 metres of the 10,000 metres even faster in 26.8sec. With these results he finally captured the elusive Olympic gold.

◀ Aleksandr Dityatin is the only gymnast in Olympic history to have won eight medals in a single Games. He was also the first male gymnast to obtain the perfect score of 10 in an Olympic competition, doing so on the vault.

◣ Cuban heavyweight Teófilo Stevenson completed his hat-trick of Olympic golds in Moscow, cementing his place as one of the great Olympic boxers.

◀ A leaflet on the protocol for the victory ceremonies.

▶ The participation medal which features the emblem of the Games was designed by Angelina Leonova.

▼ A sticker featuring Games' mascot Misha, and a call to boycott the Games.

CÉRÉMONIE
DE REMISE DES MÉDAILLES
VICTORY CEREMONY
ЦЕРЕМОНИЯ НАГРАЖДЕНИЯ

(Nom du membre du C.I.O., F.I.,
Name of the IOC, IF member,
фамилия члена МОК, МСФ)

(Sport et épreuve,
Sport and event,
вид спорта)

(Installation sportive,
Competition venue,
спортивное сооружение)

(Date et heure de la cérémonie,
Date and time of the Ceremony,
день и час церемонии)

▲ Ethiopian Miruts Yifter stormed to gold in both the 5,000 and 10,000 metres events.

1980 SUMMER OLYMPICS

BOYCOTT

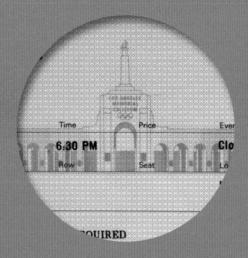

of the XXIVth Olympiad Seoul 198

Synchronized Swimming
수중발레

올림픽공원
수영경기장
Indoor
Swimming P
Olympic

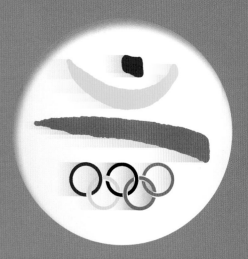

CHAPTER 5

FROM AMATEUR TO PROFESSIONAL

The Olympic Games of the 1980s and 1990s were defined by a shift from amateur, by means of financing and organization as well as with the inclusion of professional athletes. They reflected a changing world, with countries breaking up, merging and emerging to become new nations. New developments also balanced with ceremonial glamour in Los Angeles and culture in Seoul. Legacy influenced the Games in Barcelona and 100 years of Games history was celebrated in Atlanta.

Los Angeles 1984 Olympic Games

LOS ANGELES 1984

The Games of the XXIII Olympiad were a sporting and financial success, packed with loads of style and Hollywood glitter.

XXIII OLYMPIAD

Opening date: 28 July 1984

Closing date: 12 August 1984

Country of host city: United States (USA)

Candidate cities: None

Nations: 140

Events: 221

◄ The official poster for the 1984 Olympic Games was designed by Robert Rauschenberg, an American painter and graphic artist.

◢ British athlete Daley Thompson set a new Olympic record on his way to defending his title in the decathlon.

▼ Designed by C. Robert Moore of Walt Disney, 'Sam' the eagle was chosen to represent the joyful optimism of the Olympics and the national symbol of the United States.

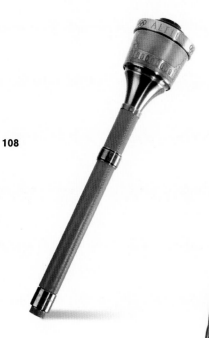

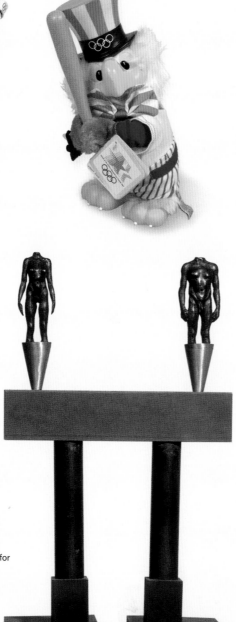

▲ The 1984 torch features the Olympic motto 'Citius Altius Fortius' and a representation of the peristyle of the Los Angeles Memorial Coliseum. The final torch bearer at the Opening Ceremony was 1960 decathlon winner Rafer Johnson.

▶ A small-scale copy of the bronze sculpture that is located at the entrance of the Los Angeles Memorial Coliseum. The sculpture was produced by Robert Graham for the Olympic Arts Festival.

Fifty-two years after the Olympic Games were first celebrated in Los Angeles they made their return in 1984 and were once again welcomed Hollywood style. The Opening Ceremony quickly set the festive tone. Even before the athletes made their entrance, the celebration was set in motion with the appearance of the 'Rocket Man', who arrived at the stadium using a jet-propelled backpack. It continued on from there with a musical extravaganza that included the use of 85 pianos and a card stunt that, with the participation of the spectators, turned the stadium into a panoramic display of the flags of all the participating nations.

Almost four hours of Opening Ceremony glamour and protocol made it clear that the Hollywood style remained undeniably intact. Even a small Soviet-led boycott could not prevent a then record number of 140 nations from taking part. Nor could a reduced level of competition in certain events stop history from being made.

◀ French pole vaulter Pierre Quinon clears the bar in the Olympic final at the Coliseum in Los Angeles to win gold.

▶ British athlete Sebastian Coe is the only runner to successfully defend a 1,500 metres Olympic title and was undefeated at the distance for seven years.

History, based both on performances and the introduction of new events, was most notably made when it came to the women's competitions. Whereas the distance of 800 metres had been perceived to be too long for women runners in 1928, at the Games in 1984 not only was an Olympic marathon for women introduced but also the first cycling event, a 79.2km (49.25 miles) individual road race. American Helen 'Connie' Carpenter-Phinney, a former Olympic speed skater, became the first female Olympic cycling gold medalist.

In the women's marathon, another American, Joan Benoit, did the same, becoming the first female to obtain the title of Olympic marathon champion. She led for all but the first three miles and ended forever the doubts about women's capacity to endure such distances. Despite the dramatic finish of another competitor, Swiss runner Gabriela Andersen-Schiess, who staggered into the stadium suffering from heat exhaustion, Benoit's time of 2:24:52 spoke for itself. It would have won a gold medal in 13 of the 19 Olympic men's marathons that had been run to that date.

In gymnastics there was both old and new as a rhythmic event was added to the artistic events for the women's competition. The rhythmic event, an individual all-around contest consisting of ball, ribbon, clubs and hoop sub-events was narrowly won by Lori Fung of Canada. In the women's artistic competitions it was Mary Lou Retton, a petite 16-year-old, who stole the show and won the individual all-around title. She also took home silver medals in the vault and team events and bronze medals in the uneven bars and the floor events.

Women also made history with the introduction of two synchronized swimming events. On the track the introduction of a women's 400 metres hurdles event proved even more historic as its winner, Nawal El Moutawakel, became both the first Moroccan athlete of either

SEBASTIAN 'SEB' COE (GREAT BRITAIN)

Sebastian Coe was a prolific world record breaker, setting eight outdoor and three indoor records. He was undefeated at both the 1,500 metres and one mile distances for seven years.

Coached by his father, Peter, an engineer, he won two Olympic gold medals in the 1,500 metres and two silver medals in the 800 metres. He also won the European title in the 800 metres in 1986.

After his competitive retirement in 1990, he served as a Member of Parliament for five years, then led the successful London bid for the 2012 Olympic Games. He chaired the London 2012 Organizing Committee and subsequently became both Chairman of the British Olympic Association and President of the International Association of Athletics Federations.

gender as well as the first Islamic woman to win a gold medal.

The standout performances in the men's competitions were celebrated as much for their links to past Olympic history as for creating new achievements.

Competing in his first Olympic Games, Carl Lewis made athletics history by matching the feat achieved by Jesse Owens in 1936, as he won gold in the 100 and 200 metres, the long jump and the 4 x 100 metres relay.

On and in the water it was a Finn, Pertti Karppinen, and an American, Greg Louganis, who matched history. For Karppinen, it was a third gold in the men's rowing single sculls event that put him on equal footing with Vyacheslav Ivanov who had achieved the same in 1960. Already a silver medallist in Montreal, Louganis climbed a spot on the medal podium in 1984, and in doing so became the first competitor since 1928 to win both the men's springboard and platform diving events.

Sebastian Coe of Great Britain won the 800 metres silver as he had in Moscow and surpassed a 16-year-old Olympic record on

▶ Special commemorative medal given to Annette Del Zoppo who worked with the firm Sussman and Prejza on the designs for the look of the Games. It makes use of the spring pastel palette with stars and confetti patterns which were also used to decorate each sporting venue.

▼ An entry ticket to the Closing Ceremony.

▶ A popular figure at the Los Angeles Games, perfect 10.0s in the floor and vault events won gymnast Mary Lou Retton gold in the all-round contest.

110

the way to becoming the only athlete to successfully defend his Olympic 1,500 metres title.

In addition to the sporting performances, the Games of the XXIII Olympiad also became known for their financial performance. Unlike previous Olympic Games, the organizers for Los Angeles faced the challenge of financing the celebration without government funding. This, however, they did successfully, as they relied instead on corporate sponsorship and made use of existing facilities such as the Los Angeles Coliseum and the athletic facilities and housing available on university campuses. So successful was their strategy that at the conclusion of the Games a profit of over US$ 200 million had been realized.

MARY LOU RETTON (UNITED STATES)

The darling of the crowds in Los Angeles, the tiny West Virginian made use of muscle power rather than aesthetic perfection for her performances. Trained by Nadia Comaneci's former coaches, Béla and Marta Károlyi, she almost missed the Olympic competition in 1984 when she had arthroscopic surgery on her knee shortly before the Games.

In Los Angeles, Retton trailed in the women's individual all-round contest with two rotations to go, 0.15 points behind the Romanian Ecaterina Szabo. Nonetheless, Mary Lou ultimately won the gold.

She never competed at another Olympic Games. Instead, despite retiring in her teens, her fame continued as she was featured in commercial endorsements and honoured with a number of distinctions including 1984 'Sportswoman of the Year' by the American magazine *Sports Illustrated*.

◄▼ In his first appearance at the Games, Carl Lewis won four gold medals in the long jump, 100, 200 metres (beating the Olympic record), and 4 x 100 metres (beating the world record). He wore these gold sprint shoes for the 200 metres event.

► The Los Angeles Olympics Games gold medal design.

▼ American race favourite Mary Decker moments before her fall in the women's 3,000 metres race.

SEOUL 1988

The Games in Seoul were a celebration of perseverance and notable upsets that not even a positive doping result in the men's 100 metres event could completely overshadow.

◀ The official poster, designed by Professor Cho Yong-je of Seoul National University, represented the Games' ideal of Harmony and Progress, the five rings symbolizing the pure Olympic spirit, and the runner carrying the Olympic torch man's progress towards prosperity.

▲ Designed by Lee Woo-Sung, the Seoul Olympic torch carries Korean motifs of the signs of the zodiac.

XXIV OLYMPIAD

Opening date: 17 September, 1988
Closing date: 2 October, 1988
Country of host city: Republic of Korea (KOR)
Candidate cities: Nagoya (JPN)
Nations: 159
Events: 237

▲ Figurines of 'Hodori', the Games' mascot, and 'Hosuni', his female counterpart, wearing traditional bridal costumes. 'Hodori', the tiger, an animal from Korean legend, symbolized bravery. His friend 'Hosuni' appeared more rarely. In Korean, 'ho' means tiger, 'dori' means little boy and 'suni' little girl.

▼ In the 1988 Games, American swimmer Matt Biondi equalled Mark Spitz's record of winning seven Olympic medals at one Games, five of which were gold.

In 1988 the Olympic Games once again returned to Asia, this time around to South Korea and the host city of Seoul. There the celebration of the Games of the XXIV Olympiad produced a mix of performance highs and lows, examples of perseverance, longevity and unexpected upsets as well as history making changes to Olympic sport.

Before the competition began, however, the world was first treated to an Opening Ceremony that paid homage to Korean tradition and a sporting hero. The Ceremony actually began as a massive Korean dragon drum was brought by procession along the River Han and then into the Stadium. Spectators witnessed displays of traditional culture but for the Korean people in attendance it was the appearance of Sohn Kee-chung that provided the most memorable moment.

MATT BIONDI (UNITED STATES)

Matthew 'Matt' Biondi, a giant of a Californian, won his first Olympic gold in 1984 in the 4 x 100 metres freestyle relay. He went on from there to win a record seven medals at the 1986 world championships and set seven world records in individual events.

With performances like these, few were surprised by his results in Seoul. There he won gold in the 50 and 100 metres freestyle as well as in all three relays. He also won a silver in the 100 metres butterfly and a bronze in the 200 metres freestyle event. The only real surprise was that he did not win a sixth gold in the 100 metres butterfly, misjudging his final stroke and losing by a mere 2.5 cm (1in).

Biondi won a total of eight golds, two silvers and one bronze medal during his participation at three different editions of the Olympic Games.

Kee-chung, who had won the Olympic marathon in 1936 competing under the Japanese name Son Kitei, was given the honour of carrying the Olympic flame into the Stadium. Once inside he passed the torch on to a young sprinter, Asian Games champion Im Chun-ae who in turn passed it on to three athletes who lit the Olympic cauldron. It was the first time that three individuals had lit the cauldron.

It is not possible to mention the sporting competitions in Seoul without also mentioning the men's 100 metres athletics race. As the world watched, Ben Johnson, a Jamaican-born Canadian, went from the high of what appeared to be a decisive 9.79-second world record breaking and gold medal winning performance to the reality of his own downfall due to his use of performance-enhancing steroids. The Games of Seoul, however, are also remembered just as much for the many outstanding performances of other athletes who competed there.

One of the most remarkable performances was achieved by Christa Luding-Rothenburger of the German Democratic Republic who won a silver in the women's cycling 1,000 metres match sprint. What made her performance so remarkable, however, was the fact that her summer performance came just seven months after she had already won a gold and a silver competing in speed skating at the 1988 Olympic Winter Games. With these two feats, Luding-Rothenburger became

◄ The running vest of Rosa Mota, winner of the women's marathon. With two kilometres remaining she attacked and won the race by 13 seconds.

▼ Prior to Mark Todd's gold medal victory in the 1984 equestrian individual eventing competition no New Zealand rider had ever placed higher than 20th. Proving it was no fluke, he retained the honour in 1988, again riding Charisma.

▶ Representing the cutting edge technology of computer manipulation, this official poster was produced using images from the 1984 Olympic Games and 1986 Asian Games.

SEOUL 1988
ATHLÉTISME
ATHLETICS

第24회 서울올림픽대회
JEUX DE LA XXIVEME OLYMPIADE
GAMES OF THE XXIVTH OLYMPIAD

the only athlete in any sport to have won medals at both the Summer and Winter Games in the same year.

For other athletes it was perseverance and surprise upsets that marked their performances at Seoul. Greg Louganis, for example, did not let the fact that he hit his head in the preliminary round of the springboard diving event and required stitches stop him from winning a second gold in the event as well as a second in the platform competition.

On the field hockey pitch play proved to be highly competitive as upsets in both the semi-finals of the men's and women's tournaments led to unexpected medal outcomes in the finals where Australia's women and Great Britain's men took home gold. In women's handball, the team from South Korea won an emotional victory over the team from the Soviet Union.

Upsets also happened in the pool where Anthony Nesty of Suriname defeated Matt Biondi in the men's 100 metres butterfly event despite the fact that Nesty came from a country that had only one Olympic-size pool.

◀ A participants' medal shows the Namdaemun, the 'southern gate', one of the masterpieces in Korean architecture built in the 14th century.

▼ The Game's highly prized Opening and Closing Ceremony tickets were, for the sake of fairness, allocated using an electronic lottery system.

▲ Map of the Olympic Park with the location and pictures of sculptures created within the context of the Olympic Arts Festival.

◢ Carl Lewis won two golds to add to the four he won in Los Angeles. He went on to win another three in Barcelona and Atlanta and was voted one of the five best athletes of the century in an IOC poll.

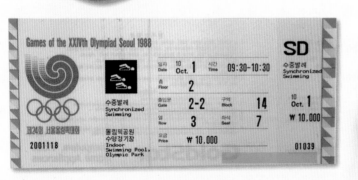

CARL LEWIS (UNITED STATES)

Carl Lewis' most successful Games was his first in Los Angeles when he won gold in the 100 and 200 metres, the long jump and as a member of the US men's 4 x 100 metres relay team. He added to his Olympic medal collection when he won two golds in 1988 in the 100 metres and long jump and a silver in the 200 metres, another two golds in 1992 in the long jump and 4 x 100 metres relay and a final gold in 1996 when he retained the long jump title.

Lewis also won eight world titles, and when he lost his world long jump crown in 1991 it was to team-mate Mike Powell. He jumped a wind assisted centimetre beyond Bob Beamon's world record but Powell jumped a non-wind assisted five centimetres beyond it and in doing so ended Lewis's run of 65 straight wins.

The distinction for longevity at these Games went to two athletes as Danish sailor Paul Elvstrøm competed in his eighth edition of the Games and Swedish fencer Kerstin Palm became the first woman to compete in seven.

It was sport as well as athletes that proved worthy of note in Seoul as tennis not only made its first appearance at the Games in 64 years, but also did so with the inclusion of professional athletes. In order to compete, however, professional tennis players had to be truly willing to embrace the Olympic experience, living in the Olympic village, absorbing the Olympic atmosphere and not just playing for Olympic gold. While reigning Wimbledon men's champion Stefan Edberg lost in the semi-final, Steffi Graf added to her victories in the year's four Grand Slam tournaments by winning the title of Olympic champion.

▲▶ Wearing these Adidas track shoes, Sergey Bubka won his only Olympic title in Seoul. He did it in some style breaking the Olympic record with a clearance of 5.90 metres.

◀ Tennis returned to the Games, bringing with it professional athletes. This allowed Steffi Graf the opportunity to win Olympic gold in the women's singles event.

▷ Overleaf: An overhead shot of the Olympic Stadium taken during the Opening Ceremony of the Games.

BARCELONA 1992

Barcelona hosted a spectacular and compact Games that left behind a legacy of facilities and roadways for the city's population to enjoy.

◄ The Organizing Committee developed a highly ambitious poster project, which involved 58 different designs. This poster carries the Games' official emblem.

XXV OLYMPIAD

Opening date: 25 July, 1992
Closing date: 9 August 1992
Country of host city: Spain (ESP)
Candidate cities: Paris (FRA), Belgrade (YUG), Brisbane (AUS), Birmingham (GBR), Amsterdam (NED)
Nations: 169
Events: 259

The Games of the XXV Olympiad in Barcelona are today remembered as much for their many notable sporting performances as they are for the emphasis that was placed on the planning for the infrastructure that was to be left behind as a legacy for the city.

It turned out to be a rich legacy that revitalized a waterfront area in need of modernization, left behind new sporting facilities and made use of an Olympic Stadium that had originally been built in 1929. Additionally, a 26-mile ring road was built and a railway line was moved to create a Games where all but four sports were largely centred closely around the hill of Montjuc and the Olympic Stadium.

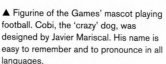

▲ Figurine of the Games' mascot playing football. Cobi, the 'crazy' dog, was designed by Javier Mariscal. His name is easy to remember and to pronounce in all languages.

▼ Torch designed by André Ricard. It moved away from traditional symmetrical shapes, adopting a contemporary style. The final torchbearers were Herminio Menendez and Juan Antonio San Epifanio. The archer Antonio Rebollo, a Paralympic athlete, lit the cauldron with an arrow.

DENG YAPING (PEOPLE'S REPUBLIC OF CHINA)

Standing a mere 1.49m tall Deng Yaping proved that height was not necessary to become a giant in the world of table tennis. Competing in her first Olympic Games in 1992, Deng won gold first with her partner Qiao Hong in the women's doubles event and then against Qiao in the women's singles event.

In 1996 Deng made a second appearance at the Games and again won gold in both the women's doubles and singles events.

Deng retired at just 24 years of age having also won 18 world champion titles. She was named Chinese female athlete of the century and has served as a member of the International Olympic Committee's Athletes Commission since 1997.

It was in the Stadium that the athletics competitions produced a number of emotionally powerful and memorable moments. In a slow paced, tightly bunched men's 1,500 metres final it was Spanish runner Fermin Cacho Ruiz who found an opening in the pack, broke free and sprinted to gold. The outcome appeared to surprise even Cacho as he repeatedly glanced back rather than looked forward to the finish line. Four years later, however, he proved it was not just luck as he picked up the silver medal in the same distance. In another event, the women's 100 metres hurdles, American favourite Gail Devers fell while Paraskevi Patoulidou stayed on her feet and by doing so became the first Greek woman ever to win an Olympic medal in any sport, and a gold one at that.

Not all of the emotionally charged moments on the track were about medals however. Spectators in the stadium and around the world watched as a father helped his son, Derek Redmond of Great Britain, make the agonizing journey to the finish line after Derek pulled a hamstring muscle in the men's 400 metres final. In the women's 10,000 metres it was the victory lap that became memorable as Derartu Tulu of Ethiopia, the first female black African to win a medal, took the lap of honour with white South African silver medalist Elana Meyer. The symbolism of this moment brought the crowd to its feet and would not have been possible without the end of apartheid and the return of South Africa to Olympic competition.

With the spires of Gaudi's unfinished Sagrada Familia church serving as the distant backdrop it should have been no surprise either that the diving events of Barcelona would long be remembered. It was not the backdrop alone that made this sport a memorable one in Barcelona, however, as 13-year-old Mingxia Fu of China won the women's platform competition by a margin of roughly 50 points. It was the first of four Olympic golds and one silver medal that she won while competing in women's platform and springboard events at three appearances at the Games.

▲▶ The admittance of professional athletes in 1988 meant that the US could submit a star-studded NBA team which included Michael Jordan (9) and Larry Bird (Patrick Ewing, 6, is in the background) for the basketball competition. Dubbed the 'Dream Team' they won gold by beating Croatia in the final 117-85. This basketball is signed by the team.

◀ Deng Yaping won two table tennis golds in Barcelona, an achievement she would repeat in Atlanta.

Fu was not the youngest participant though, as that distinction was reserved for the not yet 12-year-old Carlos Front Barrera who was the coxswain for the Spanish men's eights rowing team.

Vitaly Scherbo's entry into the Olympic history books was notable as much for his performances as for the fact that his 'nation' reflected the changing world. Scherbo put on an impressive performance as he competed as a member of the Unified Team that was made up of athletes from the former Soviet Union. He won six gold medals in the men's gymnastics competitions, including a clean sweep of the four golds available in the individual rings, parallel bars, pommel horse and vault events as well as two golds in the individual all-round and team events. In 1996 Scherbo competed in his last edition of the Games in Atlanta and there he added another four bronze individual medals to his Olympic collection.

▲ Ethiopian Derartu Tulu celebrates her victory in the 10,000 metres with silver medalist Elana Meyer. Tulu became the first woman from sub-Saharan Africa to win an Olympic gold medal.

◄ For the first time since the revival of the Olympic Games, the IOC launched an appeal for the observance of an Olympic Truce.

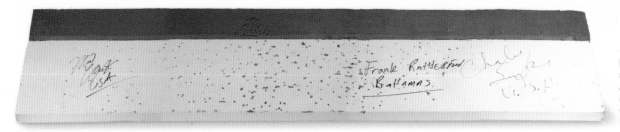

◀ The men's triple jump take-off board, signed by the three Olympic medalists. The event was won by the American Mike Conley with 18.17 metres, ahead of his team-mate Charles Simpkins and the Bahamas' Frank Rutherford.

It was no small wonder that the Barcelona men's basketball tournament is the most often remembered example of the inclusion of professional athletes at the Olympic Games. How could it have been otherwise with the American 'Dream Team' featuring such players as Earvin 'Magic' Johnson, Michael Jordan, Larry Bird, Charles Barkley and Scottie Pippen – the stuff of legends even before they played a single game in Barcelona. On the court they merely confirmed the legend as the nearest any opponent came to them was by a margin of 117-85, an achievement for Croatia in the final game.

▼ The signed competitor identification number of Vitaly Scherbo. Wearing number 24 he won six gold medals in the gymnastic events.

▼ Aleksandr Popov overcame Matt Biondi to win the 50 and 100 metres titles in Barcelona. He would go on to defend the titles in Atlanta. He was the first person to do so since 1928.

ALEKSANDR POPOV (UNIFIED TEAM)

Aleksandr Popov's coach, Gennady Touretsky, persuaded him to switch from backstroke to freestyle and used tapes shot underwater of the great American freestyler Matt Biondi to tutor Popov. In 1992 Popov, then just aged 20, defeated Biondi in both the 50 and 100 metres freestyle events. He would also win two silvers at this edition of the Games.

In 1996 Popov, who had moved with his coach to Australia to train, repeated his double and in doing so also became the first to retain the 100 metres since Johnny 'Tarzan' Weissmuller in 1928. Again he won two silver medals in the relay events as well.

Popov competed in two more editions of the Olympic Games, gaining a silver in the 100 metres freestyle at Sydney in 2000.

ATLANTA 1996

The Centennial Games were held in Atlanta where the athletes of the world were welcomed in memorable Southern style, as a then record number of nations attended and a number of new sports events appeared for the first time.

XXVI OLYMPIAD

Opening date: 19 July 1996
Closing date: 4 August 1996
Country of host city: United States (USA)
Candidate cities: Athens (GRE), Toronto (CAN),
    Melbourne (AUS), Manchester (GBR),
    Belgrade (YUG)
Nations: 197
Events: 271

122

◄ The official poster was drawn by Primo Angeli, an artist who participated in 'The Look of the Games'. He chose to present the outline of an athlete in a style inspired from antiquity.

The 1996 edition of the Olympic Games in Atlanta hold a special place in Olympic history for being the one that marked the centennial celebration. As such, they are remembered for their mixed references to their ancient and modern origins, and examples of 'Southern style' hospitality.

At the Opening Ceremony, spectators were treated to an extravaganza that paid homage to the history of the South as well as to the ancient Olympic origins. The parade of nations took longer than ever before as the Games in 1996 were notable for being the first at which all of the 197 National Olympic Committees then recognized by the IOC were present. The most poignant perhaps of all the moments of the Opening, however, was the sight of Muhammad Ali, when he struggled to overcome the shaking that Parkinson's disease brought to his hands, lifted the Olympic torch and lit the cauldron.

Another poignant moment of a very different kind came to pass just shortly after midnight on 27 July when Centennial Olympic Park, which had been designed to be a place where

◄ Olympic torch designed by Peter Mastrogiannis of Malcolm Grear Designers. It was inspired by simple ancient torches made from a cluster of reeds bound by twine. The Atlanta torch had 22 aluminium reeds, one for each previous Games, used wood from Georgia and 'The Look of the Games' elements such as the 'Quilt of Leaves.'

◥ Prototype of the Games' mascot. Originally designed on a computer by John Ryan of the local company DESIGNefx, the mascot 'Whatizit' first appeared at the Closing Ceremony of the 1992 Games in Barcelona. Its look was subsequently fine-tuned and it was renamed Izzy. The mascot appealed greatly to children, and featured in its own cartoon.

▼ The colourful 1996 Opening Ceremony included performers depicting the five coloured rings and a white dove of peace.

▲ A ticket for the Closing Ceremony that was held on 4 August in the Olympic Stadium.

◄ Michael Johnson won gold in the 200 metres with his unique upright sprint style and set a new world record of 19.32 seconds.

▼ Atlanta saw professional cyclists compete at the Games for the first time and Spanish star Miguel Indurain wasted no time in winning the gold in the individual time trial.

MICHAEL JOHNSON (UNITED STATES)

Michael Johnson was the overwhelming favourite to win the 200 metres in 1992 in Barcelona. He won 29 straight finals before June that year and was the world number one at 200 and 400 metres. Unfortunately a bout of food poisoning just days before the Games meant he was not in top form for the 200 metres and he was eliminated in the semi-finals. He did, however, pick up a gold as a member of the US men's 4 x 400 metres relay team.

Johnson made up for Barcelona in spectacular fashion four years later in Atlanta, when he set a world record of 19.32 seconds in winning the 200 metres and won the 400 in the fastest-ever sea-level time. A hamstring injury left him unable to compete with the 4 x 400 metres relay team this time around though.

Johnson, who also won nine gold medals at world championships, contented himself with competing in the 400 metres and 4 x 400 metres relay at his third Olympics in Sydney. He won gold in both.

people could gather to enjoy the festive atmosphere of the Games became a target for violence. During a concert held there that evening a bomb went off before it was possible for all those in attendance to be evacuated. Sadly, the explosion killed one person and injured another 110.

Along with these emotionally charged moments the Games of the XXVI Olympiad are also remembered for the sporting excellence of the athletes and several changes made to the number of events on the sports programme.

New Olympic events included the men's as well as women's competitions in beach volleyball, lightweight rowing and mountain biking as well as a women's cycling road time trial event. In team competitions, women's football, softball and a team rhythmic gymnastics event were also added.

In cycling, the first Olympic mountain bike victories went to Paola Pezzo of Italy for the women's event and Bart Brentjens of the Netherlands for the men's. For the bronze medalist in the women's cycling road time trial, Clara Hughes of Canada, Atlanta was just the first step in a notable Olympic career. Subsequent to Atlanta, Clara would go on to participate in one more edition of the Summer Games before she switched to speed skating and began winning Olympic Winter Games medals.

In football, the inclusion of a women's event captured the attention of the spectators as athletes such as American Mia Hamm became overnight sensations. Although men's football had first been contested at the 1900 Olympic Games, that did not stop the team from Nigeria from creating exciting new history, achieving an upset victory over pre-Olympic favourites Argentina.

124

◀ Atlanta 1996 prize diploma. A sample shown features a pictogram for athletics.

◀ Sprinter Donovan Bailey on his way to a gold medal as a member of the Canadian men's 4 x 100 metres relay team. He also won gold in the men's 100 metres.

▲ 4 x 400 metres relay baton signed by the team of the United States. The team was composed of Alvin Harrison, Derek Mills, LaMont Smith, Anthuan Maybank and Jason Rouser.

▶ American tennis superstar Andre Agassi shows off his gold medal after the men's singles event.

◀ Winner's medal. Malcom Grear Designers were in charge of refining the design of the obverse by Giuseppe Cassioli that had been used since 1928. The reverse has the Games' emblem and the Quilt of Leaves pattern.

▼ Turkish weightlifter Naim Suleymanoglu completed his hat-trick of featherweight Olympic titles at the Games in Atlanta.

American Charles 'Karch' Kiraly was an Olympic veteran who made the switch to a new discipline in 1996 when he moved from indoor to beach volleyball. The change did little to slow Kiraly down as he still managed to capture another gold to add to his two from indoors.

On the track, France's Marie-Jose Perec achieved the same 200 and 400 metres double gold as men's champion Michael Johnson. Jefferson Perez walked his way to gold in the men's 20 kilometres event, and became the first to take home a medal to Ecuador. Men's 800 metres runner Vebjorn Rodal was another athlete who achieved a first as he set an Olympic record, gained gold and became the first Norwegian track athlete to win an Olympic athletics medal.

When the athletes returned home from the Games all of them took with them their own special memories. Some, of course, took home medals as well. Unique to Atlanta was the fact that the Opening Ceremony flagbearer of each nation and each National Olympic Committee also took home a special one-of- a-kind gift, a handmade quilt that had been crafted as part of the Olympic Games Gift of Quilts project.

NAIM SULEYMANOGLU (TURKEY)

For Naim Suleymanoglu, a Bulgarian-born Turk, looks proved to be deceiving. Although he may have been short of stature and weight that did not stop this 'Pocket Hercules' from already being able to lift three times his own body weight when he was just 16 years old.

After defecting from Bulgaria and receiving citizenship in Turkey, Suleymanoglu competed for his adoptive country in his first Olympic Games in 1988. There he won his first Olympic gold at featherweight when he broke the snatch and clean and jerk world records twice each.

Suleymanoglu who retired after seeing his world title won by a Bulgarian in 1989, returned to competition where he eventually won seven world titles and two more Olympic gold medals in 1992 and 1996.

ΑΘΗΝΑ 2004

同一个世界 同一个梦想 2008.8.8 - 2008.8.24
One World One Dream 第29届奥林匹克运动会组织委员会
Beijing Organizing Committee for the Games of the XXIX Olym...

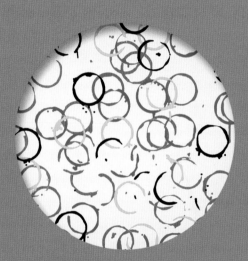

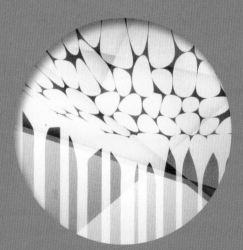

Ciclismo de pista
Cycling track

Olímpico do Rio

CHAPTER 6

MOVING INTO A NEW MILLENNIUM

In 2000 the Games moved onward, quite literally, as organizers dubbed them the Games of the new Millennium. Since then, their future has been impacted by new sports attracting new fans, increasing social media presence, new Olympic hosts and efforts to balance this magical event with global concerns. At the same time, they have marked a Greek 'return home', a three-time Olympic host and, of course, continued to highlight the sporting exploits of the athletes.

SYDNEY 2000

IOC President Samaranch's call of "Aussie, Aussie, Aussie" was answered in exuberant style 'Down Under' in a celebration that marked the passage of the Games into a new Millennium.

XXVII OLYMPIAD

Opening date: 5 September 2000
Closing date: 1 October 2000
Country of host city: Australia (AUS)
Candidate cities: Beijing (CHN), Berlin (GER),
   Istanbul (TUR), Manchester (GBR)
Nations: 199 and 4 individual athletes
Events: 300

◀ The Games emblem was incorporated in the official Games poster designed by the graphic artists of FAH Image Design. The main elements of the boomerang and the outline of the Sydney Opera House as well as the selection of colours evoke the Australian landscape. The yellow is associated with the sun, the red with earth and the blue with both the sky and the sea.

For the second time in Olympic history the Games were celebrated in Australia when the IOC selected the city of Sydney to serve as the host for the first Games of the new Millennium.

From the Games' emblem, design of the Torch and choice of mascots through to the Australian part of the torch relay and the entertainment segments of the ceremonies the rich culture and history of Australia shone through.

The Australian route of the torch relay took the flame to the sacred Aboriginal landmark Uluru as well as on its first underwater swim as a specially designed flare made it possible for the torch to be carried by a diver for a short distance along the Great Barrier Reef. Sydney Opera House, always a landmark, and the Sydney Harbour Bridge, decorated with a massive rendering of the five-ring Olympic symbol, became the backdrops for many of the cultural events associated with the Games. The entertainment segments of the Opening Ceremony included the Man from Snowy River, references to Australia's rich indigenous heritage and a nutshell history of the settling of Australia.

▲ Designed in three parts, the Sydney torch represents earth, sun and water and was inspired by the Sydney Opera House, the Pacific Ocean and the boomerang.

▶ Considered by many as one of the greatest long-distance runners of all time, Ethiopian Haile Gebrselassie won his second consecutive 10,000 metres gold medal in Sydney.

Equally memorable was the tribute that was paid to Australian women sporting legends Betty Cuthbert, Raelene Boyle, Dawn Fraser, Shirley Strickland, Shane Gould and Debbie Flintoff-King. To them went the special honour of carrying the Olympic flame into and around the Olympic Stadium before it was passed on one final time to a new generation, sprinting gold medal hopeful Cathy Freeman. As water turned to fire and Freeman's emotions were broadcast to television audiences around the world the Olympic cauldron was lit. Thus, as water cascaded from the cauldron and rose around her, the stage was set for the days of notable sporting performances that were to come.

It turned out that Freeman was not the only Australian who could turn water to fire as Sydney born swimmer Ian Thorpe, nicknamed the 'Thorpedo', also proved he could set water on fire in the swimming pool. Thorpe won gold as a member of the Australian men's 4 x 100 metres and 4 x 200 metres freestyle relay teams, another in the 400 metres freestyle in a world record time and one silver medal in the 200 metres

▼ The Olympic mascots were inspired by Australia's native species. 'Olly', a kookaburra, epitomizes the Olympic spirit of generosity. 'Syd', a platypus, represents the environment and the vigour and energy of Australia and its people. 'Millie', an echidna, is a techno-whiz and represents the information age.

▲ Australian swimmer Ian Thorpe was nicknamed 'Thorpedo' after winning three golds in the pool.

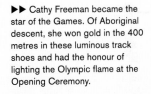

▶▶ Cathy Freeman became the star of the Games. Of Aboriginal descent, she won gold in the 400 metres in these luminous track shoes and had the honour of lighting the Olympic flame at the Opening Ceremony.

CATHY FREEMAN (AUSTRALIA)

Her father and grandfather were successful rugby league players and this Aborigine child quickly followed in the family footsteps as a sporting star. She was 16 when she won a Commonwealth Games gold as a member of the Australian women's 4 x 100 metres relay team and just 20 when she won her first individual title.

In 1996 she improved the Australian record four times until she finished second at the Olympic Games to France's Marie-José Pérec, whom she was to beat after the Games. A year later she was crowned the world 400 metres champion, a title she won again in 1999.

She entered the 2000 Olympic Games as a local favourite from whom great things were expected. Freeman did not disappoint as she won gold in the women's 400 metres race, a result that also gave her the distinction of being the first indigenous Australian to win individual gold.

129

freestyle. On the women's side it was Inge de Bruijn of the Netherlands who took home three golds in the pool, two in world record times.

In cycling it was another athlete from the Netherlands, Leontien Zijlaard-Van Moorsel, who made a name for herself. Competing in her second edition of the Games she won three golds and one silver medal in the road and track events.

In judo, Ryoko Tamura was competing in her third Olympic Games and still seeking gold. Despite the lack of gold, however, she was already a star and her result in Sydney merely elevated her to legend status. The final bout was quite literally over in little more than the blink of an eye as Tamura won her elusive gold in just 36 seconds!

The Olympic equestrian events that took place in Sydney made history just by actually taking place in Australia. They also made history when Andrew Hoy of Australia entered the record books when he won a third consecutive gold medal in the team three-day event.

History was also made as a number of new sports and events were added to the Olympic Programme in Sydney. The number of possibilities for female participants increased as events in water polo, modern pentathlon and weightlifting were included for them for the first time. In diving, both men's and women's platform and springboard synchronized events were added. Additionally, two new sports, taekwondo and triathlon were included, again with events for men as well as events for women.

▼ British rower Steven Redgrave exhales with joy after winning gold in the Coxless Fours, to make it five golds in five Games.

▲ The entry tickets to the 2000 Olympic Games included special security features such as a hologram.

STEVEN REDGRAVE (GREAT BRITAIN)

Steven Redgrave may not have been the traditional public school and university educated British oarsman but that did not stop him from becoming one of the greatest of all oarsmen, a winner in five successive Olympic Games.

Redgrave's first Olympic gold came in Los Angeles in a coxed four, the second in a coxless pair with Andy Holmes, and the third and fourth in a coxless pair with Old Etonian, Matthew Pinsent.

His fifth gold, again with Pinsent but this time in a coxless four, was made more challenging by the revelation in the year before the Games that he was suffering from diabetes that needed treatment with insulin. For Redgrave success also came at the World Championships where, between 1986 and 1999, he won at least one medal with nine of them being gold.

◀ Designed by sculptor Wojciech Pietranik, the winner's medal, displays Sydney Opera House, the Olympic torch and the Olympic rings. Winning athletes were able to have their name engraved on the obverse side, where space had been allowed for that purpose.

▼ Taekwondo appeared at the Games for the first time in 2000. This protective head gear was worn by Jae-Eun Jung from South Korea on her way to winning gold in the women's 57kg category.

▲ Tony Estanguet won gold for France in the canoe slalom singles event He would go on to defend his title in 2004 and became the first man to do so.

▼ Anti-doping sample containers similar to those used during the Games.

▶ Leaflet on how to reduce, sort and recycle waste, reflecting the Organizer's concern about ensuring a clean and green Games.

▷ Overleaf: The Sydney Harbour Bridge served as a backdrop for the sailing competitions that were held close to the heart of the city.

The success of the Sydney 2000 Olympics is in your hands

Sydney 2000 has a vision and commitment to make these Olympics the most environmentally friendly Games ever held. **Our environmental success at these games will be largely measured by the success of the waste management system**

During Games time the most important and most visual part of this system will be colour coded bins for the collection of different waste types. Approximately 80 percent of the waste produced at the Games will be back of house. **How well you sort your waste will determine the success of the waste management system.**

Look for these signs!!

| Recycled | Composted | Recycled | Landfilled | Recycled | Recycled | Incinerated |

Full details of what goes in each bin over page ➡

Measuring success

Success will be measured by the how much waste is actually diverted from landfill for recycling and composting. Putting the wrong type of waste in the wrong bin will increase the amount of waste that has to be landfilled.

Contamination

When you put the wrong waste in the wrong bin the contents of the bin become contaminated. Contamination can ruin a whole load of materials that could have been recycled or composted.

Good quality compost <u>cannot</u> be produced if the waste it is being made from has plastic, glass or metals in it. *Take the challenge – take responsibility,* DON'T put plastic, glass or metals into the deep red compostable bin.

Successful recycling depends on keeping recyclable materials separate from other wastes. *Take the challenge – take responsibility,* DON'T put food in recycling bins (yellow or blue signs). Scrape it into the deep red compostable bin.

Remember IF IN DOUBT, LEAVE IT OUT - put it in the general waste bin.

Take the Challenge - Take Responsibility

Lead by example. Share what you know with, not only your co-workers, but also spectators, athletes and anyone else who might need a hand to use the system correctly.

The success of the Sydney 2000 Olympics is in your hands.

ATHENS 2004

The Olympic flame was relayed around the world for the first time as the athletes made ready and the people of Athens and Greece prepared to welcome the Olympic Games home.

ΑΘΗΝΑ 2004

◀ The Games' official poster consists of the Athens emblem. It represents a wreath made from an olive tree branch, or kotinos, which was the prize of the ancient Olympic Games. The palette of white and blue reflects the Greek sea and sky.

▼ The Athens mascots were inspired by the daidala, a ceramic doll shaped like a bell dating from the 7th century B.C. Mascots Phevos and Athena are brother and sister.

XXVIII OLYMPIAD
Opening date: 13 August 2004
Closing date: 29 August 2004
Country of host city: Greece (GRE)
Candidate cities: Rome (ITA), Cape Town (RSA),
    Stockholm (SWE), Buenos Aires (ARG)
Nations: 201
Events: 301

The Games of the XXVIII Olympiad quite literally got off to a heart-pounding start as the Opening Ceremony began with a 28-second countdown paced by the sounds of the amplified heartbeat of a runner. The number 28 set the tone, as its reference to the number of modern Olympiads was merely one reminder of the links between the Olympic Games, Athens and Greece.

Other reminders quickly followed when the heartbeat was carried through to a dramatic drumming sequence in which the connection was made between Athens and Ancient Olympia, between the modern celebration and the first Olympic race that had been run 3,000 years before.

In a unique twist, Greece, as both the birthplace of the Olympic Games and the country of the host city, occupied the first and the last position in the parade of nations. Weightlifter Pyrros Dimas carried the Greek flag at the start of the parade and the rest of the Greek participants entered the stadium last.

The links and comparisons between Athens 1896 and Athens 2004 did not stop at the Opening Ceremony. Instead, they continued to be highlighted throughout the Games. Whereas in 1896 only 14 nations competed in 43 events, in 2004, a total of 201 nations participated in 301 events. The Panathenian Stadium, which had been renovated for the first celebration of the modern Olympic Games once again served as an Olympic venue, this time for archery competitions and the finish for the

▲ Andreas Varotsos designed the torch to resemble an olive leaf and used the philosophy of 'Pan Metron Ariston' (all things in moderation). The olive tree was often considered as sacred in ancient Mediterranean civilizations. It has long been associated with the city of Athens, and its branch is also a universal symbol of peace.

▶ US soccer star Mia Hamm was part of the gold medal-winning US team.

▼ A football shirt signed by the Iraqi football team who came fourth despite the political and military upheaval the country was undergoing at that time.

marathon races. The course of the marathon race itself followed the route that had been used for 1896 but it was Stefano Baldini of Italy who won the olive crown of victory in the men's event in 2004.

At Olympia, where the ancient Olympic Games had been held, the slopes surrounding the stadium once again filled with spectators. Times had changed, however, and those at Olympia in 2004 came to watch not only men but also women compete in their respective shot put competitions. It had been hoped that the stadium would stage the discus throw – as it had done in 1896 – but it was discovered that modern throwers' distances

▲ Russia's Yuriy Borzakovskiy celebrates as he wins the final of the men's 800 metres at the Olympic Games in Athens.

◣ Moroccan middle distance runner Hicham El Guerrouj won two golds in Athens in the 1,500 and 5,000 metres.

135

HICHAM EL GUERROUJ (MOROCCO)

It is hard to believe that with four World Championship titles in the 1,500 metres, and a nine-year performance record that included 83 wins in 89 races over the 1,500-metre or mile distance, that Hicham El Guerrouj was still searching for an Olympic gold in Athens.

The favourite to win the 1,500 metres at his first Games in Atlanta he fell after clipping the heel of the leader, Algeria's Noureddine Morceli, and finished last. In 2000, El Guerrouj again fell short of his goal, finishing second to Noah Ngeny of Kenya.

Third time lucky proved true for El Guerrouj, as in Athens in 2004 he finally captured gold in both the 1,500 and 5,000 metres, the first time in 80 years this double had been achieved.

◀ The Athens Opening Ceremony was a mesmerizing display of acrobats and dancers celebrating Greek culture.

▼ Michael Phelps set a new Olympic Games record in Athens by winning eight medals, six of them gold.

were too long for spectators to watch the event in safety, so the shot put took place instead.

Back in Athens new Olympic history was made in a variety of sports, disciplines and events that had not been a part of the ancient Olympic Games or even the first celebration of the modern Games. The men made room on the mats so that four freestyle wrestling events for female athletes could be added to the programme. Irini Merleni of the Ukraine made history as the first woman to take home Olympic gold in competitions in which a contingent of Japanese athletes showed the depth of talent on their team by capturing a medal in each of the four events.

It was not only the depth of talent on a team but also teamwork that produced results in Athens. On the basketball court, Argentina's men bounced back to win gold. A pair of divers from Greece, Thomas Bimis and Nikolaos Siranidis, demonstrated just how in synch they were, capturing gold in the men's synchronized springboard event.

For other athletes, their team-mates may have changed but this did not stop them from achieving new success with new team-mates. In the swimming pool, Jenny Thompson won her 12th Olympic relay medal as a member of the US women's 4 x 100 metres medley team. On the water, rower Matthew Pinsent won his fourth successive gold, this time in a coxless four, but without his former partner Steven Redgrave.

Athletes shone and new legends were also made in the individual events where competitors such as men's 110 metres hurdles champion Liu Xiang of China became household names. Seemingly impossible performances became possible as one of the shortest women at the Games at just 1.5m (4ft 11in), weightlifter Nurcan Taylan, lifted twice her own body weight and set two world records on her way to becoming Turkey's first female Olympic champion and British sailor Ben Ainslie proved that even after a shaky start it was still possible to come from behind when he won the Finn class yachting event by 13 points.

MICHAEL PHELPS (UNITED STATES)

Michael Phelps made history in Athens when he tied Mark Spitz's record of four individual swimming gold medals and set a Games record for a swimmer of eight medals, six gold and two bronze. So impressed were the authorities of his native city of Baltimore that they re-named a street Michael Phelps Way.

As a 15-year-old, he finished fifth in the 200m butterfly at Sydney in 2000. He followed his Athens performance by claiming eight golds at Beijing 2008, four golds and two silvers at London 2012, and at Rio 2016 he won five more golds and a silver. All in all, he is the most decorated Olympian of all time with 23 gold, three silver and two bronze medals. He also has set 39 world records, 29 in individual events and 10 in relays, the most on FINA's all-time list.

▲ Gold medal designed by Elena Votsi. The obverse shown here depicts Nike and the Panathenian Stadium, a venue of the 1896 Games.

◄ Kelly Holmes became the first woman to win the 800 metre and 1,500 metre double at one Games.

BEIJING 2008

In 2008, the Games came to China and new history was created as organizers placed their own unique mark on the event.

◀ Drawing on Chinese calligraphy, the 2008 Games emblem featured on the official poster became a new signature for the city.

▼ Made of lightweight aluminium, the Beijing torch burned environmentally friendly fuel.

XXIX OLYMPIAD

Opening date: 8 August 2008
Closing date: 24 August 2008
Country of host city: People's Republic of China (CHN)
Candidate cities: Paris (FRA), Osaka (JPN), Istanbul (TUR), Toronto (CAN)
Nations: 204
Events: 302

Beijing's Organizing Committee will forever be remembered for its 'One World, One Dream' approach and its highlighting of centuries of Chinese culture and tradition while simultaneously showcasing the city's modernity.

From the Games emblem to design elements of the Olympic torch to the five Fuwa mascots old and new were harmoniously united. The Chinese seal emblem "Dancing Beijing" subtly transformed the city's name "Jing" into an image that suggested a dancing human being. Covered in red lucky cloud graphics, the Beijing torch mixed fire with paper in a design based on a scroll. The mascots were representative of the Olympic flame and animals popular to Chinese people – the fish, panda, Tibetan antelope and swallow. In combination, their shortened names Bei Jing Huan Ying Ni translated in English to "welcome to Beijing".

When it came to venues no other embodied the organizers' wish to meld tradition with modernity better than the newly built National Stadium dubbed the Bird's Nest. A star of the Games in its own right, it was there that on 8.8.2008 at 8pm Beijing time, the number eight being symbolic of prosperity and confidence in Chinese culture, the Games of the XXIX Olympiad opened. As the world watched, hundreds upon hundreds of performers compacted 5,000 years of Chinese history into a mixture of fireworks, dancing, drumming, paddling and even a seemingly impossible flight to light the Olympic cauldron.

◀ Designed by Switzerland's Herzog and de Meuron in collaboration with China's Ai Weiwei, the iconic Bird's Nest was a challenge to build.

▼ In a stiff competition that included over 3,000 design entries it was the five FUWA that were chosen as Beijing's mascots.

JINGJING GUO (PEOPLE'S REPUBLIC OF CHINA)

Known as China's "Princess of Diving", Jingjing Guo lived up to the nickname and rewrote Olympic diving history in 2008. Competing in front of a largely home crowd the four-time Olympian and double silver and gold medallist teamed with Minxia Wu to lead the 3m synchronized springboard event from start to finish. Another strong performance in the individual springboard event earned Jingjing a second gold and a record-topping total of six Olympic medals for a female diver.

Despite talk of retirement following Beijing Guo was not yet done. In her last major competition at the 2009 World Championships she scored her fifth consecutive wins in both the women's individual and synchronized 3m springboard events.

When it came to the sporting competitions the number eight would prove to be equally fortuitous for swimming superstar Michael Phelps. With the innovatively modern and environmentally green design of the Water Cube serving as a backdrop Phelps matched his Athens total of eight medals. This time though all were gold and each was won in world record-setting time.

Not to be outdone, in the women's events it was Kirsty Coventry and Rebecca Adlington who shone. Coventry won Zimbabwe's only medals, a total of three silvers and a repeat gold medal in the 200m backstroke event. Adlington became Britain's first female swimming Olympic gold medallist since

▲ Seeded first going into the women's individual 3m springboard final Jingjing Guo continued to tally up the points on her way to gold.

◄ An autographed swimming cap that once belonged to 2008 quadruple Olympic medallist Kirsty Coventry.

► As the Games' oldest medallist at 61 years old, Ian Millar proved age was just a number in the equestrian team jumping event.

1960 in the 400m freestyle and then broke the long-standing 800m freestyle world record for a second gold.

Tennis fans were also treated to the sight of superstars as the sport's top pros battled it out. In the singles events Russian women swept the podium and Rafael Nadal realized his dream to become Olympic champion. The doubles events were a different story as Roger Federer teamed with Stanislas Wawrinka to rediscover his gold winning form and the Williams sisters Venus and Serena also bounced back to take the women's title.

In other sports other stars, heroes and media favourites emerged. Czech shooter Katerina Emmons was touted by the media as much for being the first gold medallist of 2008 as for

▲ Gold, silver and bronze. Each medal was made unique by the addition of different coloured jade on its obverse.

◄ Running shirt and race number worn by Usain Bolt during his sprint to gold in the athletics men's 200m final.

◣ With three gold medal performances in Beijing Chris Hoy was just one member of an impressively strong British cycling team.

▼ Olympic and world record setting faultless shooting gained Katerina Emmons the victory in the women's 10m air rifle event.

140

her Olympic romance in Athens in 2004. Making his record-tying ninth appearance Canadian icon Ian Millar earned his first Olympic medal at the equestrian events in Hong Kong. Not considered a rowing nation, China's gold-medal winning women's quadruple sculls team became unexpected heroes and made people change their thinking.

The list of stars would not be complete without also mentioning sprinting sensation Usain Bolt. With his distance-eating stride he made winning look easy as he raced to his first Olympic medals in world record times, and celebrated victory with his trademark archer's pose.

PETER AND PAVOL HOCHSCHORNER (SLOVAKIA)

Twins Peter and Pavol Hochschorner, or "Pepa" as they were jointly known, may be slightly separated by height and weight, but when it comes to paddling they were inseparable. Having dominated competitions for over a decade the brothers, however, credited their success to hours of training. Whatever the reason, the twins achieved what no other paddlers before them in their event had – a hat-trick of three consecutive Olympic titles between 2000 and 2008 in the men's C-2 canoe slalom.

Support for their training and celebration of their success was truly a family affair. Pepa's parents both competed in canoe slalom, their father coached them, and their sister both canoed and acted as their manager.

▲ Switzerland's Roger Federer and Stan Wawrinka display strong teamwork on their way to gold in the men's doubles tennis final.

▲ Despite placing second in both the semi-final and final runs Pepa's combined time was fast enough to earn them the gold.

LONDON 2012

Scoring an Olympic triple the Summer Games returned to London 64 years after the city last hosted the celebration.

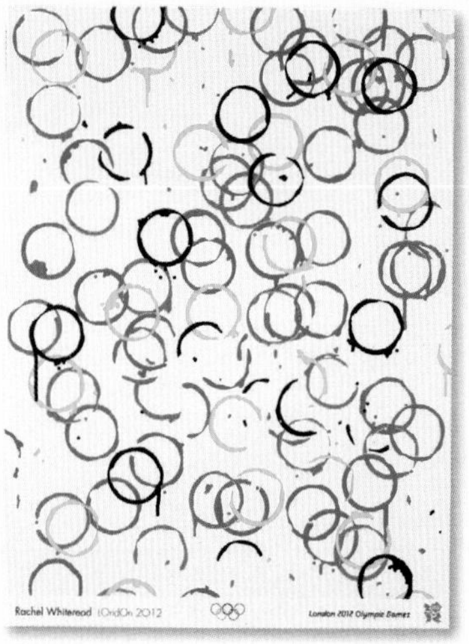

XXX OLYMPIAD
Opening date: 27 July 2012
Closing date: 12 August 2012
Country of host city: Great Britain (GBR)
Candidate cities: Paris (FRA), New York (USA), Moscow (RUS), Madrid (ESP)
Nations: 204 and 4 individual athletes
Events: 302

▲ Wenlock's design mixed London's iconic black taxi light, the roofline of the Olympic stadium and a single camera lens eye.

◤ The official poster by Rachel Whiteread used Olympic rings to suggest the celebratory gathering of athletes and spectators.

On 6 July 2005, London became the first city to be chosen to host the Summer Games a third time. But what would the Games of 2012 be like?

Unlike the 1908 and 1948 Summer Games that London hosted at relatively short notice the 2012 Organizers had seven years to plan from the time the city was elected. It was timing that permitted a plan designed to not only pay tribute to London's Olympic past but to also address Games-time and the future by ensuring an once-in-a-lifetime experience for the athletes, a focus on urban regeneration and the creation of post-Games legacies.

When the Games opened on 27 July 2012, it was in the newly built Stadium set in the newly created 560-acre Olympic Park that already showed signs of the mix of landscaped greenery, waterways, nature habitat and sporting venues that were planned to be left behind as a legacy for the future. Close by was the athletes' village, built for the Games, but destined to become housing for East Londoners afterwards. For Games time, however, the Park was home to venues for sports including aquatics, athletics, cycling and basketball.

It was there, in the Aquatics Centre, that 2010 Summer Youth

▲ The torch symbolically featured 8,000 perforated circles, one for each London 2012 torchbearer and their personal achievement.

▶ The green spaces of Olympic Park were a popular spot where spectators could relax and enjoy the Games-time atmosphere.

Olympic Games medallist Chad Le Clos from South Africa surprised even himself when he out-touched Michael Phelps to win the men's 200m butterfly. Phelps took silver and added another five medals, bringing his already record-setting overall tally to 22 Olympic medals.

At the Velodrome a new event called the omnium was introduced to test the all-around ability of the cyclists. There was both a men's and a women's competition. Contested over two days, it included one event in each of the six disciplines of track cycling.

East London was also home to a number of other competitions that took place at the ExCeL venue. There, Italy's women foil fencers proved unstoppable, capturing gold, silver and bronze in the individual event as well as team gold. It was there too that women's boxing made its Olympic debut with three events, thereby marking the first time women's events were included in all sports at the Summer Games. It was in the 48-51kg event that the first women's medals were awarded with bronze going to Mary Kom from India and American Marlen Esparza, silver to China's Cancan Ren and gold to Nicola Adams from Great Britain.

VALENTINA VEZZALI (ITALY)

At the age of six Valentina Vezzali discovered fencing. Three years later, she won her first children's trophy, and throughout her youth, World cadet and junior, as well as European junior, titles followed.

As an adult, Vezzali did not make her Olympic debut until 1996 in Atlanta. But from there she would go on to compete in four more Games editions. Nicknamed 'the Cobra' for her speed and accuracy and known for her dedication to training and sometimes passionate reactions during competitions, it is no surprise that Valentina quickly became an Olympic star. However, it was her overall tally of six gold, one silver and two bronze medals that elevated her to the status of legend and made her the most successful female fencer in Olympic history.

▲ Goggles that belonged to South Africa's Chad Le Clos who also swam to silver in the men's 100m butterfly event.

▶ A ball signed by members of Brazil's gold medal-winning women's volleyball team.

▼ These red gloves belonged to India's Mary Kom, one of the first in Olympic history to win a women's boxing medal, a bronze.

For UK fans, 4 August, or 'Super Saturday' as media called it, was a day of unending celebration as Great Britain athletes won three athletics gold medals in just 44 minutes plus three more golds and one silver in rowing and cycling events.

Not all the competition took place in East London though. Iconic London sites also hosted events.

At Wimbledon, Andy Murray was in top form in the final of the men's Olympic tennis event, giving an inspired performance and delighting the home crowd on his way to being crowned Olympic champion. 3,000 tonnes of sand were brought in to transform the Horse Guards Parade where Germany's Julius Brink and Jonas Reckermann became the first European team to win Olympic beach volleyball gold. In Hyde Park, where the triathlon both started and ended, it was anticipated that British brothers Alistair and Jonny Brownlee might cross the line together. Instead, it was the women's event that provided an incredible down to the wire finish.

Like in 1908, the Royal family could see the marathon pass below their windows, only this time it was at Buckingham Palace and not Windsor Castle. The finish line was located on the Mall rather than in the Stadium. Still, it was at the Closing ceremony, back at the Stadium in East London that the medals were awarded. Then it was time for the IOC President to call upon the world's youth to meet in four years' time in Rio, the Olympic flag to be lowered, and the Olympic flame that had burned so brightly in its 204 petal cauldron to be extinguished.

144

◀ The reverse of the winners' medals highlighted the Games emblem set against a pattern of five elements symbolizing London.

▼ Cycling shoes worn by London 2012 women's triathlon Olympic champion Nicola Spirig of Switzerland.

▼▼ Buckingham Palace was just one iconic London site that served as a backdrop for the men's and women's marathon races.

BEN AINSLIE (GREAT BRITAIN)

It may be hard to imagine that a man who named all his boats Rita could be such a fierce competitor. But Ben Ainslie is exactly that – a tough and tactical sailor. His determination has allowed him to succeed in a sport where the final outcome is often never certain until the last of the many races is concluded.

Competing in the Laser class Ben first took silver in 1996, then gold in 2000. Even after switching to the Finn class, he continued to succeed, winning the gold at the 2004, 2008 and 2012 Summer Games. Knighted by Queen Elizabeth in 2013 for his contributions to sailing, Sir Ben Ainslie has also been chosen World Sailor of the Year more than once in his career.

⬈ Ben Ainslie was all smiles after his gold medal performance made him the most successful sailor in Olympic history.

◄ A photo finish decided the gold medal in the women's triathlon, Nicola Spirig of Switzerland beating Sweden's Lisa Norden

▼ Ticket for the Closing Ceremony of the London 2012 Olympic Games.

▷ Overleaf: The delegation of every nation took home a special memento of the Games – a petal from the Olympic cauldron inscribed with the name of their country and the words London 2012.

| 12 August | 19:30 Start time | A99 Entry code |

London 2012

Closing Ceremony

Olympic Stadium
Olympic Park

Bridge: E
Block: M15
Row: 20
Your seat: 12

Account: 171
Price: £1500
Category: A
Session: ZC001

1234567890123456

RIO 2016

In 2016, the Olympic Games again broke new ground, this time going to South America for the first time. Rio de Janeiro welcomed the Games of the XXXI Olympiad to Brazil.

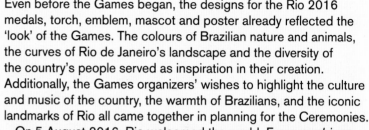

◀ The official poster features the Games emblem's inventive multi-coloured 3D design and Sugarloaf-like shape.

▼ The mascot Vinicius is a mix of Brazilian animals and is named after the famous poet of Bossa Nova.

XXXI OLYMPIAD

Opening date: 5 August 2016
Closing date: 21 August 2016
Country of the host city: Brazil (BRA)
Candidate cities: Madrid (ESP), Tokyo (JPN), Chicago (USA)
Nations: 205 plus 1 Refugee Olympic Team and 9 Independent Olympic Athletes
Events: 306

Even before the Games began, the designs for the Rio 2016 medals, torch, emblem, mascot and poster already reflected the 'look' of the Games. The colours of Brazilian nature and animals, the curves of Rio de Janeiro's landscape and the diversity of the country's people served as inspiration in their creation. Additionally, the Games organizers' wishes to highlight the culture and music of the country, the warmth of Brazilians, and the iconic landmarks of Rio all came together in planning for the Ceremonies.

On 5 August 2016, Rio welcomed the world. From *gambiarra* to *Caprichoso* and *Garantido*, to immigration and development, the Opening Ceremony melded rhythms, culture and history with moments of protocol. Symbolic paper doves carrying messages of peace fell from overhead. A kinetic sculpture backdrop reflected the glow of the Olympic flame as it burned in the cauldron and delegations from 205 nations, a Refugee Olympic Team and nine Independent Olympic Athletes paraded into the stadium ready to participate.

With the cauldron lit and the Games declared open it was time for the competitions to fully get under way. They would be contested in venues spread across four regions of Rio, as well as in five other Brazilian cities where football matches were being held.

▲ The Olympic torch reflects the colours of Brazil and its triangular shape is designed to represent the Olympic values.

▶ Fireworks lit up the night sky above the Olympic Stadium as athletes and spectators alike looked on at the Opening Ceremony, anticipating the days of competition to follow.

The region of Deodoro had the second most venues and it was there, at Deodoro Stadium, that one of those competitions quickly got started, as rugby was included on the programme for the first time since 1924. In Rio de Janeiro, though, it was the rugby sevens format that was contested, with a men's as well as a newly added women's event. The women's competition saw the Australian team making history when they gained the inaugural Olympic title by defeating New Zealand. In the men's event, the team from Fiji proved invincible. They won every match on their way to an overwhelming 43-7 victory over Great Britain in the final. It was a win that created more history as it was the first ever Olympic medal to be won by athletes representing Fiji.

The venues in the Barra region also saw the reintroduction of an Olympic sport. After an absence of 112 years, golf was back, with Justin Rose of Great Britain and Inbee Park of the Republic of Korea each scoring a competition total of 268 to become, respectively, men's and women's Olympic champions at the new Olympic Golf Course.

It was also at Barra, in the Olympic Aquatics Stadium, that Michael Phelps made his fifth Olympic appearance and added to his already record-setting collection of Olympic medals. Competing in six events, Phelps garnered six more medals, bringing his Olympic total to an incredible twenty-eight medals

▲ Brazilian school children shared what peace meant to them with spectators at the Opening Ceremony thanks to paper doves.

◄ One of the bird costumes worn by volunteers taking part in the Closing Ceremony segment presenting a bird's eye view of iconic Brazilian landmarks.

USAIN BOLT (JAMAICA)

With his ground-eating stride and signature lightning bolt pose, Usain Bolt became a star. With his never-give-up, strive-to-be-the-best attitude, he became a sprint legend.

Even early on, Bolt showed his promise by placing fifth in the men's 200m in Athens 2004. It was at the next three editions of the Games, however, that Usain found Olympic success, winning eight gold medals in the men's 100m, 200m and as part of Jamaica's 4x100m relay team. Outside the Games, he became a triple world record holder, a winner of 11 World Championship golds and the recipient of numerous additional awards.

Upon his retirement in 2017, Bolt said he would miss the competition and the fans, but not the training. It was clear fans would also miss him.

while also gaining his fourth consecutive Olympic title in the men's 200m individual medley. Despite this performance, Singapore's Joseph Schooling proved Phelps was not unstoppable. When it came time for the men's 100m butterfly, it was Schooling who captured gold, with Phelps, South Africa's Chad Le Clos and Hungary's Laszlo Cseh ending up in a three-way tie for silver.

The Copacabana region and its famous waterfront, where beach volleyball had first been introduced to Brazil, was a natural choice to locate the venue for that sport. The atmosphere within the Arena was a lively one as the German team of Laura Ludwig and Kira Walkenhorst came out on top against Brazil's Agatha Bednarczuk Rippel and Barbara Seixas de Freitas in the women's event. In the men's competition, Alison Conte Cerutti and Bruno Oscar Schmidt of Brazil battled back and forth in a tightly contested final, eventually pulling ahead to win the gold medal over Italy's Daniele Lupo and Paolo Nicolai.

With more than 63,000 spectators in attendance, Maracanã Stadium was the place to be on the penultimate evening of

the Games. A sea of yellow and green greeted the players as they started what became an exciting men's football final between Brazil and Germany that ultimately came down to penalty kicks to determine the victor. Even then, it was kick for kick until the very end, when Germany missed, and Brazil did not. It was an emotional and historic moment, as the Brazilian team won the first-ever men's Olympic football gold for the country.

Just over 24 hours later, Maracanã Stadium was again filled with spectators ready to witness another emotional moment as the Closing Ceremony began. Like at the Opening Ceremony, the music and colours of Brazil and Rio featured prominently. Before the Olympic flag was lowered and the flame extinguished, there was also time to look back on the 16 days of the Games and forward to the next celebration in Tokyo in 2020. Tribute was paid to the volunteers, the athletes' many achievements, and to the people of Brazil. Then, it was carnival time in Maracanã as the Games truly did come to an end.

▲ The single gold and triple silver medal finish in the men's 100m butterfly resulted in a rare photo opportunity for the media.

◄ It was an emotional win for members of the Brazilian football team as they earned Olympic gold in the men's event.

► British spectators were in for a treat at the last track cycling session as Jason Kenny, Laura Trott, Rebecca James and Katy Marchant all won medals.

▲ Sustainability was one of the goals for the medals' design, with recycled metals being partially used in their creation.

▶ Canadian Jennifer Kish and Fanny Horta of France in action during one of the quarter final matches in the women's rugby sevens event. Canada's team would go on to win bronze in the competition.

◣ Kaori Icho celebrates after making new Olympic history in Rio de Janeiro.

▼ Athletes competing in the men's golf competition made their mark when they signed a flag from the event.

KAORI ICHO (JAPAN)

In 2016 women's wrestling and Kaori Icho were both making their fourth appearance at the Olympic Games. For Icho, it was a moment to prove that she was back in form after an unexpected loss in January 2016 had ended an epic winning streak.

Between 2003 and 2015 Kaori had been undefeated, winning three consecutive Olympic golds and 10 World Championship titles. The question in Rio was whether she could again be victorious.

It was a tight 58kg freestyle final where Icho looked like she might be outmatched, but unwilling to give up and with less than ten seconds to go, Kaori jumped ahead. The gold was hers, and with it the distinction of becoming the first ever female athlete to win four consecutive individual Olympic titles.

TOKYO 2020

Tokyo 2020 promises to be a celebration of generations, innovation and participation as its organizers embrace new and original approaches to delivering the Games.

XXXII OLYMPIAD
Opening date: 24 July 2020
Closing date: 9 August 2020
Country of the host city: Tokyo (JPN)
Candidate cities: Madrid (ESP), Istanbul (TUR)
Events: 339

▲ The 2020 Games mascot Miraitowa's name was selected to promote a future of eternal hope, and its design incorporates the blue ichimatsu moyo patterns of the Games emblem

◤ Designer Asao Tokolo's Games emblem for Tokyo 2020 combines three rectangular shapes to represent the diversity of cultures, countries and ways of thinking.

On 24 July 2020, Tokyo will welcome the world for a second time. Fifty-six years after Tokyo first hosted an edition of the Olympic Summer Games, venues such as the Nippon Budokan and the Yoyogi National Gymnasium will be reminders of 1964, as they again serve as competition sites for a new generation of athletes. The Games in 2020, however, will in many ways reflect their growth and evolution – changes that are about much more than an increase in the number of participating nations and athletes, or the expansion of the sports programme and number of events contested, versus those at Tokyo 1964.

As a candidate city for 2020, Tokyo presented their vision for a future-focused edition of the Olympic Games that would be innovatively designed to 'Discover Tomorrow', as well as to celebrate both the Olympic values and those of the Japanese people. It was a vision that Tokyo was given the opportunity to turn into reality when, on 7 September 2013, the International Olympic Committee elected the city to host the Games of the XXXII Olympiad over the other candidatures of Madrid and Istanbul.

▲ The 2020 torch, created by Tokujin Yoshioka, features the Games emblem and a traditional Japanese Sakura-mon cherry blossom shape, from which the Olympic flame will burn.

▶ The Tokyo 2020 candidature also had an emblem; one that combined the colours of the Olympic rings with the purple traditionally used during the Japan's Edo-era festivals and events.

In the time since Tokyo's election, the Organizing Committee, city and citizens throughout Japan have all had a role in seeing the vision take shape. Even before the passage of the Olympic flag from the Mayor of Rio de Janeiro to the Mayor of Tokyo, and its arrival on Japanese soil, the countdown to the Games had already started and would continue. Celebrations to mark 'to go' milestones such as 2020 days, three years, 500 days and even one year have built up anticipation for the start of the Games. These milestones, as well as a four-year cultural Olympiad and other initiatives planned by the Organizing Committee, have highlighted sport, art, culture and engaged the public.

The nation's youth, technology and sustainability, as well as the IOC's Olympic Agenda 2020 recommendations and elements of 'new', have also been highlighted in the planning and preparation the Organizing Committee has undertaken for the Games.

In the planning and build-up to the Games of the XXXII Olympiad, Japan's younger generation has had a variety of opportunities to participate. Through the 'Creating Tomorrow Together' project, school children could express their dreams for 2020, and a 'Yoi Don' programme focused on educating students about the Olympic Games and their impact is also part of the Organizing Committee's plans. '2020 Young Athletes' has engaged aspiring athletes and given them a role in a project designed to emphasize education and the Olympic values. In addition, school children also had a role in such initiatives as the selection process of the Olympic mascot and planting the flowers that will be used at the spectator entry points to the venues.

▲ Even Olympic athletes joined in the launch of the initiative to create the 2020 medals from old electronics metals.

◀ The first ever coloured coin issued by the Japanese mint celebrates the Olympic flag handover ceremony.

▼ Planning is a joint effort as Tokyo 2020 Organizers and the IOC Coordination Commission meet to review progress on Games preparations.

153

◀ As part of the advance celebrations for the 2020 Olympic Games a young fan has a chance to experience sport climbing.

▼ The Organizers' focus on sustainability is reflected in this souvenir bento-type meal box featuring manga characters popular in Japanese culture.

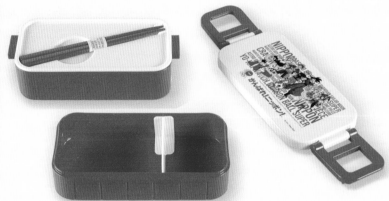

◀ Tokyo Governor Yuriko Koike proudly carries the Olympic flag upon its arrival in Tokyo following the handover ceremony at the Closing of the 2016 Games in Rio de Janeiro.

▶ Supporters gather to celebrate the '2020 days to go' mark in the planning for the Games of the XXXII Olympiad.

▼ A souvenir badge featuring the Tokyo 2020 emblem and a maneki-neko 'lucky cat', popular in Japanese culture.

It is not, however, just the younger generation, or even the Japanese population in general, that have been provided with an opportunity to have a role in the Games. Thanks to technology, the 80,000 volunteers will be joined by robots that will greet athletes and guests at Olympic venues and offer assistance to spectators in wheelchairs. Those not attending the Games will also have a chance to be part of the experience. Social media will be used, via 'Make the Beat', so that individuals from around the world can post selfie videos that might end up being shown on the big screens at the competition venues during the Games.

Technology has even been incorporated into the designs for the Olympic torch and medals, which have also been designed to embrace the Olympic Agenda 2020 recommendation on sustainability. For the torch, innovations have been included in the combustion design and the aluminium from post-earthquake temporary housing has been given a second life by being used as the metal casing. People throughout Japan will have the opportunity to say that they made a contribution to the creation of the Olympic medals. Gold, silver and bronze collected from discarded or obsolete electronic devices, such as mobile phones, digital cameras and laptops that have been donated by the public, will be processed into the pure metals needed to produce the Olympic medals.

But advances in technology and an increased emphasis on sustainability are only one part of what is new with this edition of the Games. The programme has also been changed as a result of the first-time application of the Olympic Agenda 2020 recommendation that an Organizing Committee could propose additional sports for their edition of the Games. For Tokyo 2020, this has meant a process whereby 18 events in five sports – karate, skateboarding, sport climbing, surfing, and men's baseball/women's softball – were approved by the International Olympic Committee. An archery team event, a men's and women's competition in 3x3 basketball, and BMX freestyle have been added to the sports programme, as well as new mixed events including a 4x100m medley relay in swimming, a 4x400m relay in athletics (both teams being two men and two women).

Their inclusion takes into account traditional and emerging sports that are both locally and internationally popular, and have youth appeal. They are sure to lead to the writing of new Olympic history as the Games unfold in Tokyo.

159

PICTURE CREDITS